My Health, My Faith, My Culture:
A guide for healthcare practitioners

Other books from M&K include

Spiritual Assessment in Healthcare Practice
ISBN: 9781905539277

Nurses and Their Patients: Informing practice through psychodynamic insights
ISBN: 9781905539314

Managing Intimacy and Emotions in Advanced Fertility Care:
The future of nursing and midwifery roles
ISBN: 9781905539079

Perspectives on Death & Dying
ISBN: 9781905539215

The Primary Care Guide to Mental Health
ISBN: 9781905539109

Research Issues in Health and Social Care
ISBN: 9781905539208

A Pre-Reader for the Foundation Degree in Health and Social Care Practice
ISBN: 9781905539680

Identification and Treatment of Alcohol Dependency
ISBN: 9781905539161

Perinatal Mental Health: A clinical guide
ISBN: 9781905539499

The Clinician's Guide to Chronic Disease Management for Long-Term Conditions:
A cognitive-behavioural approach
ISBN: 9781905539154

My Health, My Faith, My Culture:

A guide for healthcare practitioners

Sue Timmins

My Health, My Faith, My Culture:
A guide for healthcare practitioners
Sue Timmins

ISBN: 978-1-905539-80-2

First published 2012

British Library Cataloguing in Publication Data

A catalogue record for this book is available from the British Library

Notice

Clinical practice and medical knowledge constantly evolve. Standard safety precautions must be followed, but, as knowledge is broadened by research, changes in practice, treatment and drug therapy may become necessary or appropriate. Readers must check the most current product information provided by the manufacturer of each drug to be administered and verify the dosages and correct administration, as well as contraindications. It is the responsibility of the practitioner, utilising the experience and knowledge of the patient, to determine dosages and the best treatment for each individual patient. Any brands mentioned in this book are as examples only and are not endorsed by the publisher. Neither the publisher nor the authors assume any liability for any injury and/or damage to persons or property arising from this publication.

To contact M&K Publishing write to:

M&K Update Ltd · The Old Bakery · St. John's Street

Keswick · Cumbria CA12 5AS

Tel: 01768 773030 · Fax: 01768 781099

publishing@mkupdate.co.uk

www.mkupdate.co.uk

Designed and typeset by Mary Blood

Printed in England by Ferguson Print, Keswick

Contents

About this guide

All patients, irrespective of their cultural background and religious affiliations, may have particular needs relating to the provision of their healthcare. Every patient is entitled to a delivery of care which is sensitive and person-centred, and which allows them to retain dignity. A reflection by healthcare practitioners of these requirements, based on the chosen or birth faith of their patient, must be an integral part of that patient's care delivery. Where the healthcare practitioner has an understanding of those potential requirements, an appropriate care plan can be identified to help to meet those needs, to support compliance, and to ensure that the patient's wishes are complied with wherever possible.

This entitlement was first outlined in 1991 in **The Patients' Charter** (Department of Health (DoH), 1991) and subsequently in **The Patient's Charter and You** (DoH, 1996):

> '...patients can expect the NHS to respect (their) privacy, dignity, and religious and cultural beliefs at all times and in all places.'

The White Paper **The New NHS: Modern, Dependable** (Secretary of State for Health (SSfH), 1997) subsequently stated the intention that everyone in the nation would have

> '...fair access to health services in relation to people's needs, irrespective of geography, class, ethnicity, age or sex'.

It further stated that the 'renewed NHS' would deliver 'a personal service which is sensitive and responsive to the needs of individual patients'. The NHS has been working towards these objectives in recent years, and the latest White Paper, **Equity and Excellence: Liberating the NHS** (SSfH, 2010), further develops this theme.

It is therefore important that all healthcare practitioners have access to resources which will help them to increase their awareness of cultural and religious issues, and which demonstrate to them how this information may improve their delivery of care to their patients. It is recognised that:

> '...knowledge of a patient's culture can provide the health professional with some insight into the meaning of individual behaviour in illness, and improve the quality of care provided. Recognition by staff that [a patient] from a minority group may have different concepts about health and illness, as well as different expectations

from consultations and care delivery, will go a long way in winning the confidence [of the patient], and ensure compliance with advice and treatment.'

(Hopkins and Bahl, 1993)

In this guide, the term 'minority groups' is used to indicate cultural and racial groups who have their origins in countries other than the United Kingdom (UK). These groups might therefore include, for example, Southern Irish, and the traveller population, as well as those people who may be identified more superficially by, for example, features or skin colour. Religious affinities apply both to people from immigrant stock and to those who may be described as 'indigenous white British' who have by choice adopted or converted to faiths other than the State faith of Christianity (in any of its forms). Equally, it must be borne in mind that the many branches of Christianity have differing views about certain clinical interventions and procedures, and that followers of any religion may adhere to its strictures with varying degrees of compliance, under differing circumstances.

In many rural parts of the UK, the host population is known to be in the majority; however, continuing numbers of people from elsewhere in the world enter the country, either settling by choice near their places of entry, or moving to be near established family groups, or relocating elsewhere under dispersal programmes. There are also many people from the host population who follow religions other than Christianity, either from birth or from personal choice.

In order to deliver appropriately-designed and sensitive services, healthcare practitioners should be aware that all patients may have specific healthcare needs, either due to cultural or religious rules or preferences, or because of recognised genetic predispositions to certain medical conditions. As indicated above, this may not only apply to patients from minority ethnic groups but also to those members of the host population who follow faiths other than Christianity.

Where there is a large minority population in one geographical area, levels of awareness of potential cultural and religious requirements are often relatively high. On the other hand, however, there are many rural areas where the perceived minority population is low in number, and consequently the need for awareness of issues relevant to these patients is not always seen as a priority. This can mean that, in local areas of the country, healthcare continues to be delivered professionally, but may not always be tailored specifically to be sensitive to the needs of individual patients.

Research in primary care in one area of the UK (Timmins, 2000) revealed that, in rural areas, some primary care practices had good levels of awareness of these specific needs, with a resulting ability to meet them; however, the general level of awareness amongst the practices surveyed was relatively low. Many practices reported that they had not at that stage identified a need to provide culturally sensitive services, and some asked for help in developing this aspect of their service delivery.

Many healthcare practitioners working both in the NHS and in the private, independent and voluntary sectors may have had little direct exposure to people from other lands or to non-Christian faiths, and this guide is intended to act as an introduction to these topics. It is particularly intended for those healthcare practitioners who are less familiar with the religious requirements which may affect person-centred patient care, so the guide covers the major world religions, including Christianity, in order to offer a useful overview and comparison. The guide is also intended to act as a reference document for those seeking guidance and information, in order to assist all personnel to offer an appropriately sensitive healthcare service to all their patients, irrespective of those patients' backgrounds or faiths.

This guide will assist healthcare professionals to recognise and value the differences which may be encountered when patients of other faiths, whose potential needs may be less familiar to them, present in the healthcare setting. Other reading material, much of which has informed the compilation of this guide and which may also be of interest to the reader, is listed in the References and Bibliography sections at the back of this book.

About the author

Sue Timmins MSc, DMS, AssocCIPD, MIHM

Sue has a background in management, initially in industry, and subsequently within a variety of healthcare settings, including experience in a Postgraduate Medical Centre, six years as a Hospice Administrator, and, since 1997, in the NHS as Kent and Medway GP Staff Training Manager, responsible for commissioning and delivering education and training to all personnel employed in GP practices across the Kent and Medway Cluster area.

Sue's interest in the cultural and religious influences in healthcare has grown over the years, influenced by both personal experience and her time working in palliative care. Her Masters dissertation explored the ability of GP practices in a local area to deliver care, which is appropriately tailored to the needs and wishes of patients with differing cultural backgrounds and religious affiliations. This research highlighted the need for specialist training and for suitable information to be readily available to all healthcare staff. She has also lectured on this topic as part of a university Spiritual Care module.

Part 1 | Culture, religion and health

Introduction

Chapter 1

Healthcare – patients' rights and expectations

Primary healthcare was originally defined in 1978 by the Declaration of Alma Ata as:

> '...essential healthcare made universally acceptable to individuals and families in the community by means acceptable to them, through their full participation and at a cost which the community and the country can afford. It forms an integral part both of the country's health system of which it is the nucleus, and of the overall social and economic development of that community.'
>
> (World Health Organization, 1978)

As already mentioned, the 1997 UK Labour Government White Paper **The New NHS: Modern, Dependable** (SSfH, 1997) stated clearly the intention that everyone in the nation shall have:

> '...fair access to health services in relation to people's needs, irrespective of geography, class, ethnicity, age or sex. For example, ensuring that black and minority ethnic groups are not disadvantaged in terms of access to services.'
>
> (ibid., section 8, para. 5.ii)

It also stated that the then 'renewed NHS' would deliver:

> '...a personal service which is sensitive and responsive to the needs of individual patients...'
>
> (ibid., section 7, para. 1)

Prior to the publication of that White Paper, **The Patient's Charter and You** (DoH, 1996) had indicated to patients that, under the terms of the Patient's Charter (DoH, 1991, subsequently revised in 1995 and 1997), they had a right to be treated fairly, irrespective of race, religion, or colour. **The Patient's Charter and You** was available in many languages in the UK, thus enabling this information to be accessed by many non-English speaking members of the population. A greater awareness of their rights therefore raised patients' expectations that their particular needs should at least be recognised, even if they could not always be met immediately by individual practitioners. The Patient's Charter was itself abolished under the terms of the NHS 10-year plan in 2001, but the principles of fairness and equality of access to healthcare were established by its original publication, and were further clarified in the **NHS Constitution for England** (DoH, 2010).

The Constitution defines certain rights for NHS patients, including:

NHS Main Principles:

The NHS provides a comprehensive service, available to all irrespective of gender, race, disability, sexual orientation, religion or belief (DoH, 2010, p. 3).

NHS Values:

You [the patient] have the right to be treated with dignity and respect, in accordance with your human rights (DoH, 2010, p. 6).

Professor the Lord Darzi of Denham also commented in **High Quality Care for All** that (referring to the NHS):

> 'It is also an excellent opportunity to pursue our duties to promote equality and reduce discrimination under the Equality and Human Rights Act.'
>
> (DoH, 2008a, p. 21)

He further states throughout the document that patients have an increased expectation of personalised care, and the right to be treated with dignity throughout.

The latest Guidance for primary care doctors from the General Practitioners Committee (GPC, 2011), on the subject of overseas visitors and their eligibility for primary healthcare services, advises that primary care practices must not discriminate on grounds of religion or ethnicity (among other criteria) and must provide emergency treatment to any person within their practice area, but it is at their discretion whether or not they register that person as a patient. Asylum seekers (referred to in a later section of this guide) may be able to produce an Immigration Service application card, but it is emphasised that a practice asking for identity or immigration status must ask the same question of all patients. Asylum seekers are entitled to NHS primary medical services without charge, and the link to the Table of Entitlement can be sourced through the GPC document referenced above. The determination to an entitlement for free treatment in secondary care is not the responsibility of the referring primary care practice; this is the responsibility of the secondary care provider.

The ethnic composition of the population of the United Kingdom

There is little doubt, in the early decades of the third millennium, that the UK is a multicultural country. From the beginning of our history, our shores have proved a magnet to people from other lands, many of whom settled here. Some were seeking to extend their own countries' boundaries, some were fleeing oppression overseas, and others had land gifted to them by royal patronage. Indeed, in past centuries, England itself used to 'own' large areas in Northern France, to say nothing of the colonies across the world over which the country had sovereignty in the days of the British Empire. The origins of the majority of the resident population are mixed, beginning with pre-Roman times, through the Anglo-Saxon and Viking eras, and subsequent political and familial European alliances from the Middle Ages onwards.

In more recent times, the ethnic composition of the UK has continued to change. For hundreds of years, there have been pockets of inhabitants whose origins or religious beliefs are different to the indigenous majority; for example, in England, sailors from the Indian subcontinent settled in Kent, in the Medway Towns and in Thanet; there was an established Muslim community in Liverpool; there has for some time been a Filipino community on the Romney Marshes. In Sussex, there are small but significant Somali, Arab, and Iranian populations. This picture is not unusual, and is replicated all around the country, with large immigrant populations to be found, for example, in the port cities of Bristol, Liverpool, and Grimsby, as well as in the major conurbations like Manchester, London, Glasgow and Birmingham.

Although the historical pattern of immigration to these shores was limited in earlier times, much of it has taken place since the beginning of the 20th century. In particular, a considerable number of people from Caribbean countries were invited to the UK after the Second World War (1939–1945), to fill the British labour market (Watson, 1977; Squires, 1991; Karmi, 1996). Asian immigration also developed at that time, when men who had joined the British Armed Forces overseas settled in Britain and subsequently sent for their families to join them here. Some years later, Asian immigrant families arrived in large numbers during the 1970s. Entire communities were expelled from Uganda in the early part of that decade by the regime of Idi Amin; they dispersed to many countries across the world, including the UK, where many of them already held the acknowledged right to British citizenship.

It is also acknowledged that, for example, travellers and European Union (EU) nationals also require regular medical attention whilst in the UK, and thus their potential cultural and religious needs must also be recognised and addressed.

The 1991 Census indicated that the ethnic minority population of the UK was then 5.9 per cent of the total population (at just over 5 million out of the total population of approximately 55 million people) (Karmi, 1996); the 2001 Census subsequently reported that the percentage had risen to 7.6 per cent (ONS, 2002a) (4.5 million out of a total of 58.8 million (ONS, 2002b)). No question about religious affiliation was included in the 1991 Census, and the reply to the question in 2001 was voluntary. The March 2011 census also included a voluntary question about respondents' religions.

The results from those who volunteered their religion in 2001 (93 per cent of total respondents) showed that the population of England alone (given as 49.1 million people (ONS, 2002c)) reported their religion as:

- 75.97 per cent Christian (37.3 million people)
- 3.1 per cent Muslim
- 1.1 per cent Hindu
- 0.7 per cent Sikh
- 0.5 per cent Jewish
- 0.3 per cent Buddhist
- Non-respondents – 7.7 per cent (4,011,000 people)

(ONS, 2002d)

(The remaining 10.6 per cent is not recorded for the purposes of this analysis.)

It is acknowledged that these percentages of stated non-Christians include converts to religions other than Christianity from within the indigenous population, as well as those born into the respective faiths.

In major conurbations throughout the UK, such as in Birmingham, where 13.9% of the population in 1997 was of Pakistani origin (Runnymede Trust, 1997, p. 14) or Bradford, 9.5% (ibid.), a Muslim patient visiting his local health centre or being admitted to hospital might reasonably expect that some of the healthcare professionals caring for him might be of the same faith. They might also possibly share a similar cultural background; if not, they might have easy access to information about the requirements of his religion and culture, through published or local guidelines and/or local and national NHS chaplaincy services.

Rural communities are very different, having smaller pockets of population, and with many areas of recognised deprivation. Healthcare practitioners in these areas may know that they have very few patients from minority ethnic groups. In some areas where there is no perceived need for this information, patients registering with a new family doctor may not be asked whether they have particular religious affiliations. Where health centres and primary care providers recognise that they have 'minority group' patients on their lists, these patients may be perceived, accurately or not, to have become 'Westernised' or less compliant with the requirements of their religion or culture, and thus therefore may not be perceived as requiring culturally sensitive care. Due to this limited exposure and, frequently, to the previous lack of specialist training provision, the situation for healthcare practitioners may have been that they had no formal mechanism for familiarising themselves with the particular needs of patients following different religions, and having varying ethnic origins.

Nationally within the UK, it is now recognised that the needs of minority groups are an issue for consideration within the overall range of the health needs of the population. Particular sensitivity should be fostered towards their different needs. Local and national initiatives now demonstrate that work has been undertaken, and continues to be prioritised, to remove all barriers to healthcare, including those relating to ethnicity and religion.

Culture and health

Several publications have been produced over recent years about the healthcare needs of the immigrant population; many of these refer specifically to their requirements and preferences when being treated in the acute or secondary setting. The need for sensitive treatment of patients with specific cultural or religious needs in primary care, and in the whole of the private, independent and voluntary sectors, is no less great. An awareness of the needs of people with differing backgrounds is essential for all healthcare practitioners, and even if a patient shares cultural or religious affiliations with the healthcare practitioner, their levels of compliance may not be the same. The requirement for healthcare personnel to become aware of these needs was recognised by the UK Government in the late 1990s, and was referred to in the White Paper **The New NHS: Modern, Dependable** (SSfH, 1997), and was later reinforced with the report **The Future of Multi-Ethnic Britain** (Parekh, 2000), thus forming a firm foundation for future service design. These public documents emphasised that the training of healthcare practitioners in cultural awareness is absolutely essential, and endorsed this observation, which was made some years earlier:

> **'Education – at least to the level of basic awareness – on the needs of minority groups should be an essential part of preparation for all those who plan to work in health care.'**
>
> (Bahl, 1993)

Healthcare professionals will be familiar with the epidemiology of the residents of their own local catchment area. The local demography will also be known, and most healthcare practitioners can describe broadly their practice profile. This profile is based on the patient population, and the conditions and diseases endemic to those people. Their health is affected by many factors, amongst which are income levels, housing, employment status, education, and diet.

These same factors affect everyone in the world. All patients, wherever their origins, are affected by their individual diets, personal beliefs and circumstances, as well as by their cultural backgrounds, and, possibly, by the dietary and normative requirements of their religious practices.

People with different cultural backgrounds may also handle their illnesses differently. As an example, people from the Asian subcontinent may present with stomach pains. These pains may possibly not be gastric in origin; Asian patients are known to somatise mental stresses into digestive disorders, and these may often be treated by recognising that counselling, or the ability to discuss problems openly, rather than treating the symptomatic stomach disorder, may improve that patient's general health.

It is important that the healthcare professional understands these factors, since a patient may present for diagnosis or treatment with symptoms of illness which it is possible to misdiagnose, if that professional is not familiar with the possible options. All healthcare personnel need to be aware of the differences; we are not all the same in our presentation of illness. Language difficulties for non-English speakers, or for patients for whom English is not the first language, may also make it less easy for those patients to convey how they feel, and the need for an efficient interpretation service for all patients is recognised and recommended.

A patient's cultural background has a great influence on their health. Just because an illness is traditionally treated with what might be described as 'folk medicine' does not mean that the condition could be better treated with conventional medicines. Many Eastern people believe that food and drink have 'hot' and 'cold' properties, influencing different body parts and symptoms, and believe therefore that eating certain foods will cure or assist specific conditions (Karseras and Hopkins, 1987). Likewise, religious practices and prohibitions must be recognised by the healthcare practitioner as being of utmost importance to the patient (Spector, 1991). 'Different' is not necessarily 'wrong', just because it is unfamiliar. A health visitor suggesting that an Asian mother should wean her baby onto proprietary foods in jars may cause consternation, when for generations the babies in that family have been weaned on naan bread and mild curries, preparing them for their preferred spicy diet in later life.

Cultural and religious issues may affect minority group patients from cradle to grave. Neile (1997, p. 118) comments that 'a service is only relevant if it caters for the perceived needs of the population which is using it'. She quotes as an example the fact that a woman from an ethnic minority group may not attend ante-natal classes if the information and advice given there differ from her cultural norms. Religious issues apply equally in these situations.

At the end of life, religious communities may have particular requirements for the cleansing and laying to rest (by whichever is the preferred method for that faith community) of the body of one of their number. As an example, Gatrad (1994) cites the difficulties which Muslim patients may face when a family member dies. Muslims prefer to die in their own homes, amongst their family and others of their faith. He describes the difficulties which Muslim families often encounter in obtaining speedy death certification, in order to comply with their religious requirement that a dead person should be buried as quickly as possible. He adds that post-mortems are not allowed within Islam; it is accepted that, in the United Kingdom, this may be demanded by the law, but this can cause further delay and distress to relatives.

The link between culture and religion is strong, and is indistinguishable in many parts of the world (Henley, 1979). Again taking Islam as an example, the behaviour of society in Muslim countries is based on religious teachings which cover every aspect of life and social interaction. It is often difficult for the Westerner to distinguish those aspects of behaviour which stem from religious beliefs, and those which have developed over time in people's native countries or districts. Practising Muslims will follow Islamic codes of conduct irrespective of where in the world those people originate, or where they now live. Westerners may erroneously perceive this way of life as, for example, 'Arab' or 'Pakistani', according to the origins of the person under discussion. A British Muslim woman may adapt traditional British garments to comply with the Islamic requirement for modest dressing. In the same way, people from other lands will follow religious and traditional ways of life which accommodate their individual native circumstances. The healthcare practitioner must always bear in mind that the religious and cultural norms of the immigrant and indigenous populations are equally worthy of consideration and respect.

In many ways, people entering and settling in this country have influenced British society throughout history, and have become an integral part of the British way of life – international cuisine is found on our high streets. However, the cultural issues and behaviours of individual minority groups are still frequently misunderstood, and many of the difficulties still experienced by those groups in healthcare matters may arise from the ignorance or uninformed prejudice of individual practitioners. Sometimes, misunderstandings can be simply resolved by discussion and explanation; intervention at an early stage can prevent expressions of anger, frustration and dissatisfaction from both healthcare practitioner and patient. For example, a patient declining to take medication in capsule form may not be being difficult; there may be a genuine understanding that capsules often contain gelatine, which as a pork or beef by-product is prohibited to Jews and Muslims, and Hindus, respectively.

In comparatively recent times, vegetarians were sometimes mocked by their carnivorous fellows; it is not so very different to follow a kosher (Jewish) or halal (Muslim) diet, but these are nevertheless perceived as 'foreign' by many native British people, and treated with some suspicion. It is a point of discussion to note that the Jewish people, who number many less than the Muslim community in the UK, are generally better accepted, possibly because they tend to dress in Western styles, and do not therefore appear 'different' to the onlooker (Watson, 1977).

Ineffective communication can be a barrier to effective healthcare. For example, the historical fact that older first generation women from the Indian subcontinent rarely spoke good English continues to present considerable problems in areas such as women's health, where many people still remain unaware of the availability of screening programmes (first discussed by Kubba, A., in Rawaf and Bahl, 1998). This problem is also replicated in the transient refugee and asylum seeker populations. However, in recent years, much has been done to address this issue, with outreach health services going direct into those communities, and many information leaflets about available services now being published in many languages relevant to local populations.

Language difficulties also arise in consultation, where much can be lost in translation, due to lack of understanding (Ahmed, 1998). Basic comprehension about the workings of the human body cannot be assumed of any patient, irrespective of background or origin, and limited knowledge, combined with differences in terminology and phrasing, can lead to considerable misunderstandings. Healthcare professionals will be aware already that when giving advice or instruction to anyone, it is essential to check verbally that these have been understood. This is particularly important in situations where the patient has limited grasp of spoken or written English. It is not sufficient to ask questions which merely require 'yes' or 'no' answers; clarification must be sought as to the course of action which the patient is to take. A health visitor or paediatric nurse examining an unwell baby may ask the mother whether the baby has been sick. The healthcare professional intends to ask whether the baby is vomiting; 'sick' to a mother with poor English may merely mean 'unwell', and, if inaccurate terminology is being used in this conversation, inappropriate diagnosis, advice and treatment might then result.

In some areas, the needs of the elderly immigrant are poorly addressed; many of the elderly speak limited or no English, and many still find it difficult to understand that native Britons may treat the older generation very differently from the way that they would expect in their birth country (Admani, 1993). One example of potential unmet health and social care need is that elderly Asian patients are sometimes restricted to their own homes through their inability to communicate for themselves, and many may still have a high incidence of rickets, due to their lack of exposure to sunlight, limiting their access to naturally occurring Vitamin D. Because they remain in their homes, they do not interact with their host neighbours, and thus may remain isolated within their own families (Oram, 1997).

To attempt to circumvent translation difficulties, many areas of the NHS negotiate interpretation contracts with agencies such as Language Line and Migrant Helpline, under which the majority of languages can be interpreted, either as a three-way telephone conversation, or in person at the consultation.

Refugees and asylum seekers

The UK's national constitution is such that it recognises the needs of people from all over the world who are in fear of their lives from persecution on religious grounds. Subject to their being able to prove their case, the UK has always welcomed refugees and asylum seekers, be they Huguenots fleeing from France and Northern Europe, German and Polish Jews seeking refuge from Nazi oppression, British Asians expelled from Uganda under the Amin regime, or Iraqis and Somalis fleeing war and insurrection in their respective countries.

The picture began to change rapidly at the end of the 20th century when simmering discord once again flared up into war in the former Yugoslavia, and Serb Christian forces began a programme of ethnic cleansing against the Bosnian (largely Muslim) population. Thousands of people of all ages and states of health began to enter the UK's sea and air ports, both by legal and illegal means. Due to government policy at the time, the majority who claimed asylum on landing were initially housed near their ports of entry, resulting in large numbers of people being allocated accommodation in, for example, south Kent and the Medway towns, as well as in major cities with international ports and airports.

To illustrate the numbers of incoming potential patients requiring healthcare at that time, and the effect on the ability of local services to manage them, the then East Kent Health Authority reported that in March 2000, 3600 asylum seekers were registered with local doctors, and that approximately 25% of these were unaccompanied minors. These high numbers were undoubtedly due to the location within that part of the UK of the sea ports of Dover, Folkestone and Ramsgate, with ferry services arriving daily from Europe, and the Channel Tunnel Shuttle freight services at Folkestone, and a Eurostar passenger station in Ashford. Specific asylum seeker services had to be set up in the county to deal with the influx, and with their particular needs. In later years the picture began to change, as admitted refugees and asylum seekers were dispersed elsewhere throughout the UK after initial screening.

The healthcare services offered by the asylum seekers' facilities were delivered so as to be acceptable to people from many differing ethnic and religious backgrounds, and offered interpretation facilities. This provision ensured that asylum seekers were able to access and use fully the local NHS services, including screening.

The immigration process itself may cause health problems in many people. They may find themselves alone in the host nation, and may find that they are required to settle in communities which are potentially hostile, and where their customs and needs may not be understood or tolerated. It is important therefore that the indigenous population recognises that, although economic migrants undoubtedly exist, many of those seeking access to asylum in the UK may be fleeing genuinely from oppression, torture, and religious intolerance. Many of the people on our streets, who have applied for asylum in the UK, may be well-qualified professional people in their own countries. Both refugees (and indeed, all immigrants) and the host population need to be aware that their cultural norms, and consequently their behaviour, may be different, and misunderstandings can therefore arise.

It may be helpful to healthcare personnel to describe here the various recognised rights of residency under which the population of the UK is classified. The following are useful definitions:

- Citizens, who have a legal right to residency in this country. Cohen (from whom these definitions are cited) states that citizenship is 'a basis for leverage within State institutions for pursuing appropriate resources for their needs';
- Denizens, who have right of residency or domicile, but who have not been granted citizenship. This group of people may travel in or out of the country at will, and may be making considerable contributions to the country's economy;
- Helots, who include illegal immigrants, and asylum seekers whose right to stay in the host country has not yet been determined. The current system for determining the right to asylum can result in some helots being resident in the UK for a number of years before their cases are considered and resolved.

(Cohen, 1994)

Anyone from these groups may seek healthcare treatment under the NHS. Although this population may be transient, the NHS still undertakes to offer free healthcare to the refugee population (GPC, 2011). Eligibility criteria are notified to healthcare organisations through regulatory documents from the Department of Health and other interested organisations (DoH, 2011; GPC, 2011). The 'Vulnerable Migrants' pages of the Health Protection Agency document (HPA, 2011) provide useful information and links specific to the potential physical and mental health needs of this group of patients.

It is acknowledged that the refugee community of all ages may need urgent mental healthcare. Many in recent years have suffered appalling levels of deprivation or torture and fear, either in their homelands or in transit, and have reached the shores of the UK under very difficult conditions. Immigration officers are not medically trained, and initial symptoms of illness may go unrecognised (Karmi, 1998). Some of the refugee women are pregnant, in the mistaken belief that this will advance their eligibility for housing and other benefits (Downing, 1999).

On a social level, refugees are not always welcomed by less well-informed local people, since they may be perceived as a drain on local resources and funding; the refugees are often unwell due to their experiences mentioned above, and they seek treatment in local primary care practices. Once there, issues about the healthcare system may well arise; for instance, they will be unfamiliar with the processes in the NHS system, and, through language and cultural differences, they may fail to appreciate relatively simple issues such as the importance of keeping to timed appointments in the healthcare system. Language difficulties can also lead to non-compliance.

To counteract and surmount these difficulties, a basic understanding amongst healthcare practitioners of the situation of the refugee and asylum seeker population will assist them in formulating a sensitive approach to this particular patient group.

Intolerance and prejudice – assimilation or integration?

Ahmad and Atkin (1996) commented that the population of the UK has traditionally thought of itself as being a tolerant society. They went on to say that this view has been challenged since the 1950s, when the first waves of immigrants entered the country, brought in to work by the then government. The Ugandan Asian influx of British citizens in the early 1970s fuelled a wave of underlying and overt racism, which has been evident from time to time ever since as a recurrent theme, refuelled in recent and current times by fear of terrorism and extremism. Disaffected members of the minority groups may be involved, and immigrant groups may dispute amongst themselves; the Handsworth riots in Birmingham in the 1980s were between Asian and Afro-Caribbean people, at that time resentful of each other's positions in the local communities.

It may be assumed that, in order to settle down and build a life in their new country, first generation immigrants desire to be accepted by the host population whilst still retaining links with their places of origin. This continued contact, and desire to remain in touch, often causes conflict. Birth country influences can be very strong, particularly where they are founded on religious practices, and there is an overwhelming desire that these should not be forgotten or abandoned. Strong links often remain with their birth country, with members of their family often remaining there (Watson, 1977), and extended return visits are often made when this can be afforded. Many immigrant workers have immediate family in their home countries and send a large part of their pay home to their relatives. Split loyalties can result, with immigrants feeling a strong need to assimilate themselves into their new community by conforming to the norms of the host country, but wishing sincerely to retain and practise the culture of their family origins. This need to conform, to assimilate and become like those already in the host country, may be strong, but nevertheless the culture from the home country (even for second and third generation immigrants) remains strong and colourful, and may be reflected in their domestic settings. Although the majority of immigrants recognise and adhere to the law of their adoptive country, there is no way that they would wish to deny their cultural and religious origins (Constantinides, 1977; Joly, 1995).

A prime example of this is the often-misunderstood practice of arranged marriages. Although forced marriages are unacceptable, and are now against the law in the UK, the arranged marriage, when conducted properly, can be an admirable process for all concerned. The concept – that both families of the intending participants are fully involved and can satisfy themselves that their family backgrounds, social standing, standards and lifestyles are compatible – gives them confidence that their respective offspring will commit themselves to a union in which they will not encounter unexpected cultural or social demands, and which is fully supported by their families. In cultures in which divorce and extra-marital relationships are unacceptable, a firm foundation is thus established from the outset. Because of the demands of the parental 'wish list', it is frequently the case that suitable marriage partners are not found within the UK population of that particular minority group, and in these instances the partner is then sought in the homeland amongst family and friends still resident there.

This single example indicates that, in one area of life alone, the process of integration requires considerable understanding and input from the indigenous population of the host country. It should be anticipated that the newcomers may be different, and they should be valued for that difference. True integration will come when the whole community can acknowledge each other's lifestyles and beliefs without embarrassment or intolerance, recognise the value of diversity in the population, and embrace the way in which newcomers to the shores of the UK enrich its national culture. However, in practice, the newcomers have often been perceived as a threat to the 'British' way of life, and rather than being welcomed, they have been ignored or ostracised.

It is not surprising, therefore, that minority groups are often more comfortable with situations which are familiar to them, or where they can be assured of a certain level of sensitivity. McAvoy and Donaldson (1990) stated that, at that time, and since the late 1950s, some 24% of doctors in the NHS had come from outside the UK, and approximately 84% of these were of Asian origin. A primary care practice with Asian doctors is likely to attract Asian patients, particularly if they are the only such primary care facility in the locality.

It is important that healthcare professionals recognise that certain ethnic groups have a predisposition to certain illnesses and clinical conditions. Instances of these conditions are, for example, that diabetes and coronary heart disease are more prevalent amongst the South Asian population (e.g. Raleigh *et al.*, 1997; Radha and Mohan, 2007); genetic conditions such as sickle cell anaemia are endemic in black people with African or Afro-Caribbean origins (Chapple and Anionwu, 1998); and thalassaemia is another condition affecting many people from Asia and Africa. The recognition of the possibility of these predispositions may assist healthcare professionals to identify and diagnose previously unfamiliar conditions in their patients.

Inequalities in health

It is recognised that a large proportion of the immigrant population lives in relative deprivation. In the early years of the 21st century, it was stated that 'one-third of the officially homeless are drawn from ethnic minority groups' (East Kent Health Authority, 2000, p. 14), and 'people from minority ethnic groups are at a greater risk of violent crime and of racial harassment' (ibid., p. 15). Many have little understanding of their rights to welfare benefits and services which might improve their standards of living (Ahmad and Atkin, 1996). It is also noted that higher numbers of immigrants are likely to be found in areas of high population and social deprivation.

Where there is deprivation, there is poor health, irrespective of background and ethnicity. Economic and cultural issues, as well as ethnic and religious considerations, must be taken into account when planning health services (Tovey, 2000), and current government and Department of Health policies and publications endorse the fact that there must be no discrimination in access to services.

Whilst planning suitable services and strategies, healthcare providers must remain aware that the definition of cultural differences is not exclusive to people of other countries; there are many different cultural divides between people within the UK, emanating from differences such as income, employment status, housing, education, and social class. Differences between healthcare practitioners and their patients in the perception of any situation must be set aside if clinically effective healthcare is to be delivered, and the same provision must be made for the immigrant and convert population.

The identification (ideally at the time of joining a primary care practitioner's list, or of registering for other healthcare interventions) of patients from differing ethnic minority and religious groups may assist healthcare professionals in planning future services, and in particular in recognising potential health and future needs (Tovey, 2000).

The success of local implementation of the national and local initiatives, supporting the message of equality of access to healthcare for everyone, will depend on the ability of all healthcare practitioners to deliver appropriately-designed care to meet the needs of all individuals, irrespective of their origins and beliefs.

The original research behind the production of this guide

Primary care, and in particular, general medical practice, is usually the first point of contact with the NHS for the majority of patients. It is frequently stated that 80% of all clinical interventions take place within primary care, and this will be sustained and will increase with the current drive for patients to be treated closer to home under primary care Commissioning Consortia arrangements, described in **Equity and Excellence: Liberating the NHS** (SSfH, 2010).

Research in 2000 (Timmins, 2000) investigated the ability of primary care practices in a large rural area, with perceived low numbers of patients from minority groups, to deliver appropriately-tailored and sensitive care to any patient who might present from any minority ethnic or religious group. This was measured by assessing the basic levels of understanding of all personnel in participating surgeries, including the medical personnel, about various aspects of ethnic minority cultural and religious life, and their potential effects on the delivery of healthcare. The research revealed the following results, amongst the surgeries surveyed:

- There were a number of surgeries, headed by doctors who were themselves from differing cultural and/or religious backgrounds, where the staff were well-informed, and to whom patients requiring recognition of, and adherence to, specific practice would gravitate.

- There were surgeries serving areas in which universities and other internationally-recognised centres of education were situated, and where overseas students were admitted, which were well-informed and able to offer appropriate services to their patients.

- Conversely, many participants had little or no knowledge of the needs of minority groups. They reported that they had very few or no such patients on their lists, and believed that this was an unlikely prospect. However, the future arrival of one such minority family in their catchment area, with particular needs, might mean that those needs might not be met with sensitivity, since the staff might be unaware of their cultural origins and/or preferred norms, which might affect the success of any healthcare interventions.

- Even where the awareness of individual members of staff was declared to be limited, it had been expected that primary care doctors, as independent contractors and employers within the wider NHS, would have access for themselves and their staff to the sources of appropriate literature and resources regarding the needs of patients of different faiths and cultures. The responses from the participating surgeries at that time indicated that this was not always the case.

Equipping healthcare providers to deliver appropriately sensitive care

In the past, it could have been stated that the National Health Service in the UK was slow to respond over the years to the changing needs of minority ethnic and religious groups, irrespective of their origins. The government White Paper **Health of the Nation** (SSfH, 1992) first highlighted the importance of addressing the health needs of people from ethnic minorities. Balarajan and Raleigh's subsequent work for the Department of Health (1993) makes specific reference to the then ethnic minority population of the UK, and to the morbidity and mortality patterns attaching to specific groups within that population. Subsequent government documents have built upon those foundations.

Patients' perceptions of the ideal sensitive and responsive healthcare service may, however, be quite different in practice. Neile (1997) quotes from Weller (1991), who stated that:

> '...[the NHS] remains essentially geared to the attitudes, priorities and expectations of the majority population, which is considered white, middle class, and nominally Christian.'

Ahmed (1998) then commented that:

> '...current healthcare provision is based upon Western medical models, which do not reflect the beliefs, values and attitudes to health held by minority ethnic communities.'

Several years later, in 2008, a paper from the National Library for Health identified that satisfaction with the NHS was then still perceived as low amongst patients from minority groups, largely because the collection of data on ethnicity was patchy, and the proposal then was that monitoring data should be collated centrally. The paper reported that the gypsy and traveller population was a highly marginalised minority ethnic group, and awareness-raising projects were proposed (SLEH, 2008).

However, despite these earlier observations and initiatives, the Government White Paper describing the latest planned reforms in England and Wales acknowledges that:

'…The NHS also scores relatively poorly on being responsive to the patients it serves. It lacks a genuinely patient-centred approach in which services are designed around individual needs, lifestyles and aspirations. Too often, patients are expected to fit around services, rather than services around patients.'

(SSfH, 2010, para. 1.9)

The White Paper goes on to describe its vision for a future NHS in which this situation will be improved:

'We want the principle of 'shared decision-making' to become the norm: no decision about me without me. International evidence shows that involving patients in their care and treatment improves their health outcomes, boosts their satisfaction with services received, and increases not just their knowledge and understanding of their health status but also their adherence to a chosen treatment.'

(ibid., para. 2.3)

Regarding end-of-life care, it states that the government will:

'…introduce choice in care for long-term conditions as part of personalised care planning. In end-of-life care, we will move towards a national choice offer to support people's preferences about how to have a good death, and we will work with providers, including hospices, to ensure that people have the support they need.'

(ibid., para. 2.20)

However, these ambitions assume that the patient understands their role in this partnership, and has the right tools and information to participate fully. A past report from the then Director of the NHS Ethnic Health Unit (EHU) (NHS Confederation, 1998) found that many patients from minority ethnic groups did not know that they have a right to ask for an interpreter, and that therefore family members were often used for this function. The report also found that where good practice existed, it depended upon doctors and other healthcare professionals using whatever resources were then available to them, to enable them to provide sensitive services. That report particularly commented that:

'…all members of the primary healthcare team require training. This is particularly true of front-line staff, to enable them to provide culturally sensitive care…and female health professionals to examine women patients.'

The work produced by the EHU suggested that at that time, throughout the country, minority patient groups were:

'keen to work with the NHS at all levels. Their requests for service provision are practical and modest in terms of resources.' (ibid.)

The EHU recommended that the following specific improvements were then needed – they referred particularly to primary care medical practice, but it could be inferred that this reflected also into other parts of the NHS at that time:

- All members of the primary healthcare team should have access to training in cultural and religious awareness.
- Patient information should be available in foreign languages appropriate to local patients.
- Female health professionals should be employed, to examine female patients.
- Robust and available interpretation services should be easily accessible.

The research undertaken (described in the previous section) evidenced that some of the lessons learned had not then been reflected fully in the healthcare system, in rural parts of the UK. The overall picture regarding levels of awareness of minority cultural and religious issues amongst healthcare staff can still be improved. The levels of awareness identified can be described on a scale from 'highly aware, and able to deliver a sensitive service' to 'not aware, and delivering a service which meets the needs of the indigenous population, and is therefore assumed to meet the needs of any minority patients which we may have'.

Since that earlier report, many inpatient units have introduced a variety of improvements which acknowledge the diversity of their patient populations. Many sites have multi-faith prayer rooms which adhere to no particular following but which can provide appropriate literature and artefacts if required; in some settings, the direction of Mecca is marked on the wall or floor (alerting their Muslim patients to the direction towards Mecca, for their prayers). Many hospitals and hospices have resident chaplains who have easy access to ministers and leaders from a range of faiths who are able to visit patients, and provide support and advice to the healthcare teams caring for them.

Education and training

It is acknowledged that for all clinical staff, including the medical profession, training in cultural issues should ideally form part of their pre-qualification training programmes (Karmi, 1996) and investigation with leads of pre-registration programmes at a number of universities shows that this is now the case. However, non-clinical staff may have very little opportunity to undertake a suitable level of awareness training. McAvoy and Donaldson (1990, p. 36) recognised that:

> '...there really is little point in the clinical members (of the team) enhancing their capacity to help (minority) patients, when all is undone by patient-contacts with receptionists or secretaries who have not had this training… this is an immensely sensitive area of staff development…'

Individual healthcare employers, and the personnel whom they employ, can make considerable inroads into improving access for patients from minority groups, and to improving the sensitivity of care which those patients receive.

The report from Lord Darzi emphasised the importance of education and training for staff, in delivering a person-centred package of care:

> 'High quality care for patients is an aspiration that is only possible with high quality education and training for all staff involved in NHS services. They provide care in a changing healthcare environment.…Patients and the public, quite rightly, have increasing expectations of personalised care.'
>
> (DoH, 2008a, p. 78)

The companion paper on the workforce, issued alongside the Darzi report, further emphasised education supporting the patient-centred focus:

> 'The skills for listening, understanding and responding to the needs of individual patients and supporting them to manage their health in a manner that is respectful

of diversity and difference must, wherever possible, be incorporated into education and training programmes and clinical practice.'

(DoH, 2008b, p. 13)

Recognising these recommendations, many of the universities and other organisations providing pre- and post-registration clinical programmes of professional education and training now include culture and diversity topics within their curricula. The recognition of cultural and religious diversity is a thread weaving through programmes before professional registration, and an important part of post-registration specialist modules (author's personal written communications with: London South Bank University, 6 December 2010; Canterbury Christ Church University, 26 December 2010; University of Greenwich, 17 January 2011).

For many staff employed in the health and social care sectors, attendance at equality and diversity training sessions will be part of their core and mandatory training programmes. It will be desirable if, in future and when commissioning services, the commissioners ask for this training to be evidenced by all provider services, so they can ensure that all patients will receive culturally sensitive treatment, should the need arise.

The NHS Core Learning Unit e-learning programme 'Equality and Diversity' is one example of an on-line awareness-level training programme available free of charge to NHS employees (Skills for Health, 2011); there are many other commercial training providers able to deliver suitable programmes, where the need is identified.

Publications which will prove valuable additional reference tools for all healthcare personnel include the following.

- **Religion or Belief: a practical guide for the NHS** (Department of Health Equality and Human Rights Group, 2009)
- The UK Health Protection Agency's Migrant Health Guide, available on their website **http://www.hpa.org.uk/MigrantHealthGuide/**. These on-line pages offer many useful web links for healthcare practitioners to develop their knowledge and understanding, both for themselves and for the education of their patients. Specific enquiries can also be raised on-line via this site.

Local documentation

The original research previously mentioned revealed that many primary care surgeries did not at that time ask new patients whether they had any particular religious affiliations, although for many minority group patients, this will form an integral part of their daily life (Henley,

1979). This is therefore an important question, which should ideally be asked at the outset when registering patients at all healthcare facilities. It is possible that this point would be raised later when treatment is necessary, but it is equally possible that it may not be considered at all, because the healthcare provider has not yet recognised that this is a useful piece of information to record.

When the NHS Electronic Summary Care Record (ESCR) is implemented fully, data such as this should then be available immediately on-line about the patient at any healthcare facility linked nationally, and any religious affiliation noted. The NHS Connecting for Health website has a report on the current scope of the project (Connecting for Health, 2011). At this early stage of implementation, the ESCR for England and Wales only shows the patient name, date of birth, and registered primary care practice, and shares basic clinical information i.e. medical conditions, allergies and medications (personal communication with PCT Connecting for Health training manager, 10 March 2011). However, although practices may ask for religion and/or ethnic background when signing up a new patient, this information does not yet appear on the ESCR when shared with other organisations (personal communication with a primary care practice manager, 11 March 2011) – this information may be added at a later stage of implementation of the project, under the Enrichment process (personal communication with PCT Connecting for Health training manager, 10 March 2011). It is therefore suggested that until consistency in new registrations is in place, adherence to accurate and comprehensive local records should be a requirement for all new patients.

This situation might not present a problem to non-religious or non-observant patients, or to those following religions where most medications and their presentations, and medical interventions, are generally acceptable. Certain religions, however, forbid their followers from eating and drinking certain substances, and have very strong views about certain medical interventions (Karmi, 1996). Several common medications presented in capsules may be formulated with the pork by-product, gelatin, which Muslims and Jews may not consume; likewise, certain liquid medications have an alcohol base, which is forbidden by many religions. Particular care should be taken with the religious prohibitions of certain patients, for instance in treating diabetic patients; Hindus (to whom the cow is sacred) will not accept beef insulin, and Muslims and Jews (with a prohibition against pork) will find pigs' insulin unacceptable. Apparent cases of non-compliance with medication in these patient groups may therefore be resolved by a change of prescription to something which is acceptable to the patient. In addition, the practice of fasting on certain days must also be taken into consideration when prescribing or recommending oral medication.

It can also be significant, particularly in an emergency or in case of imminent or actual death, for the healthcare practitioner to know whether a patient requires particularly sensitive terminal care and treatment on religious or cultural grounds (Karmi, 1996).

Healthcare providers who are unaware of the cultural and religious backgrounds of their patients may run the risk of believing that cultural awareness is not relevant to them when planning healthcare services. For instance, an opinion that the raising of cultural issues during family planning training is irrelevant to an individual practice population presupposes that healthcare professionals in that practice may be treating every patient in the same way, disregarding through lack of awareness any personal (and possibly unvoiced) needs which the patient may have. All patients may have personal or cultural preferences about contraception. Any patient, irrespective of background, who feels that they have no choice or does not know that they have healthcare choices, may not ask for special consideration, and many might be reticent in being outspoken about a potentially delicate subject such as this.

A presupposition that a healthcare provider which currently has no minority group patients does not need to educate its staff in at least the basics of this important topic, is an insular view, although it is recognised that healthcare providers have to decide their individual priorities for themselves. It must however be remembered that primary and secondary care is expected to deliver a sensitive service to all patients, and it cannot be assumed that any one healthcare provider will never have a patient from a minority group on its lists.

Patient information documentation

Information and guidance about services available to patients also needs to be reviewed regularly. Many healthcare facilities already provide information leaflets in a wide variety of languages and formats, but may be reliant on being sent relevant documents, and some may only provide a very limited range. Even if individual sites do not keep an up-to-date store of leaflets and resources, it is important that they know where to obtain them, or how and where to access translation facilities in order to produce their own information in languages appropriate to their patient population.

However, even this may not address the problem entirely. The provision of leaflets and reading material either in English or in a variety of other tongues presupposes that all patients are able to read; it is however understood that many first-generation immigrants, and some of the indigenous population, either have poor literacy or are illiterate in their own languages. Many of the Asian languages have very specific dialects known only in small regions of their home countries. It is therefore essential in all patient interactions to make sure that the patient, or the person providing translation, fully understands the terminology being used, and the instructions and recommendations being given to the patient. Without clear communication channels, patients with a poor command of English will not experience the equality of access to healthcare services which was first envisioned in **The New NHS: Modern, Dependable** (SSfH, 1997) and subsequent publications.

Consultations

Another area which must be included in the improvement of the delivery of sensitive patient care is the area of the consultation itself.

Irrespective of their ethnicity or religion, many patients receiving healthcare may have a preference whether they see a male or female practitioner. Many women, irrespective of background, prefer to see a female doctor or nurse for advice on obstetric or gynaecological matters. This issue becomes very important for communities such as Muslims, where women are reluctant to expose their bodies in public to other women, and are forbidden by their religious code from exposing their bodies to men other than their husbands (Henley, 1979). The preference for single-sex consultation may apply equally to Asian men, who may additionally have a cultural aversion to being seen by a female nurse, as nursing was at one time considered a low-caste activity on the Asian sub-continent (ibid.).

The topic of chaperon(e)s is equally important to all patients, irrespective of their origins, and should also be a priority for healthcare professionals themselves. There have been serious and well-publicised cases in the recent past where male medical practitioners have been accused of indecent assault whilst conducting examinations on their female patients; as a result, many doctors in healthcare facilities (both in primary and secondary care) now prefer to be chaperoned when conducting intimate examinations. Difficult situations may also arise between male patients and female nurses, or potentially, in same-gender intimate consultations.

Training for chaperones is now available in many locations, and the benefits of the service are reiterated during the training, and details included of how to report poor practice if need be; the role of the chaperone is to protect the interests of all involved in the consultation. In many primary care surgeries, this option should be available to both patients and staff, and notices about the service are often prominently displayed. The facility may not always be requested or used, but it is available, and can be actioned promptly when required.

Offering equality of access to healthcare services in these ways can be a problem in smaller healthcare facilities, for instance a primary care practice where all the doctors are of the same gender (and this can apply equally to group practices or single-handed surgeries). Research (Timmins, 2000) reported that 25% of surgeries surveyed advised that a patient had declined to join their lists because only doctors of one gender were available to them. Patients are therefore disadvantaged if they are unable to consult a healthcare professional who is acceptable to them on cultural or religious grounds, and this disadvantage can be replicated across the whole spectrum of patients.

Interpretation facilities

The question of interpretation can present an issue to healthcare facilities with patients who have little or no command of the English language. Many such patients will therefore not understand what is being said to them, even if the conversation is slow and clearly enunciated (conference notes, 2000). Many primary care practices subscribe to professional translation facilities, but many healthcare organisations also confirm that the practice of using family members for interpretation is widespread (Henley, 1979). Care must be taken in these instances, firstly to ensure that the questions and the patient's answers are accurately translated by the person interpreting, and secondly that possible prejudices, or embarrassment on the part of the amateur translator, do not affect the interpretation. On both cultural and religious grounds, it is not always seen as appropriate in certain minority groups for a husband to attend a consultation if his wife has gynaecological problems, and it is felt indelicate if a child does so. Breaches of confidentiality can also arise with the use of family interpreters (NHS Confederation, 1998).

It is not uncommon for family members to be used to interpret for indigenous patients who are deaf. The same issues arise for minority group patients, and it is not clear whether there are in fact sufficient foreign language interpreters, who are also fluent in sign language, available to healthcare services, to meet this particular situation should it arise.

Interpretation is recognised as being an area fraught with difficulties, and although there may be no perceived language problems in some healthcare facilities, there may well be unrecognised and unmet cultural norms and religious requirements, due to inadequate interpretation facilities.

Forms of address

Some of the more common naming systems are described under the appropriate sections of this guide. Since patients of many religious backgrounds may be registered for healthcare, it will be perceived to be a sensitive approach to all concerned if registration forms and other documents refer to 'first' or 'given' names, rather than 'Christian' names. It is likely that the majority of people from other faith groups will understand the reasons behind the term 'Christian name' within the UK; nevertheless, the origin of the expression is clearly that this is the name with which a person is Christened, i.e. baptised into the Christian faith. To recognise diversity and to avoid any possibility of discrimination, an alternative form of reference to first or given names is desirable.

Similarly, some cultural groups may be unfamiliar with the expression 'surname', preferring the option of 'family name'; however, as will be seen later in this guide, this too can be open to misunderstanding in those cultures where several members of the same family group bear different name structures.

Healthcare practitioners also should be aware that in some cultures, e.g. patients of Oriental background, the first word in their name may be their family name or surname, with their personal name following behind. It is therefore worth checking the name by which the patient wishes to be known, and how it should be recorded on the patient's records.

Religious beliefs

The guide gives information about several faith groups, and about the practices and norms which followers of those faiths may wish to observe. It is important to remember that people who profess faiths may be more or less observant than the next person sharing that faith. Some people may be more relaxed about the norms and requirements of their religion than their neighbour, but their potential religious requirements must still be acknowledged.

Research in primary care in part of south-east England (Timmins, 2000) revealed that primary care practices may have patients on their lists who are believed to follow a number of different religions, and it is those religions which are referred to in this guide as being prevalent across the UK. It is recognised that it is not an exhaustive guide, and the author welcomes comment from healthcare practitioners who can identify other areas of faith and culture which should be explored and included in any later editions of this guide.

It must be remembered that it is not only people from ethnic minority groups who may follow religions other than the British state faith of Christianity. At one time there may have been a perception that the indigenous population is 'White Anglo-Saxon Christian', but this has changed over recent years. Many people of white European and American origin follow alternative religions, and faith cannot be determined, or even guessed at, by skin colour alone. The same criterion applies to all people; religious and cultural affiliations cannot be pre-assumed simply by comparing them to others of apparently similar origins or to other groups of similar outward appearance.

Questions which you might like to ask yourself prior to a consultation

- Has the patient given me their full name?
- Do I understand the composition of the name?
- Has the patient indicated how they would like to be addressed?
- Does the paperwork in the healthcare setting indicate 'Christian' name? If so, will this mean anything to a patient following another religion?
- Will this patient wish to have a clinical examination by a healthcare professional of the same gender?
- Will this patient (or do I) wish to have a chaperone present during any examination?
- Will I need interpretation facilities? If so, do I know how to access them?
- Do I understand the significance of this patient's jewellery and/or clothing?
- Does this patient have dietary preferences or prohibitions?
- Are any medications or clinical interventions prohibited to, or disliked on grounds of faith by, this patient? It is important to ask, if I am not sure.
- Is it possible that the patient is fasting?
- If the patient is pregnant, is there anything special which I should know about their preferred birthing arrangements?
- If the patient is dying, is there anything special which I should know about their end-of-life wishes?
- If the patient is bereaved, do I understand the rituals which they will wish to follow?

Most patients will be pleased to be asked about these matters, and to have their dignity and wishes taken into consideration. Just because someone does not ask, it does not mean that they have no wishes – they simply may not realise that it is possible for their wishes or preferences to be realised.

Summary

Although many healthcare facilities throughout the UK are undoubtedly delivering highly appropriate services, many minority group patients in areas where their population is low in number may be receiving a healthcare service which, by default, is not a 'personal service… sensitive and responsive to the needs of individual patients', because the healthcare practitioners delivering the service may not be fully aware of the specific potential requirements of patients from different cultural or religious backgrounds. Although progress has been made in recent years, many organisations may not yet be offering fully the equality of access described as 'fair access to health services in relation to people's needs, irrespective of geography, class, ethnicity, age or sex'. These requirements were first outlined in the White Paper The New NHS: Modern, Dependable (SSfH, 1997), as national standards for the delivery of equitable healthcare to the entire population of the UK, and these foundations for standards have been built on in subsequent government papers and reports referred to earlier in this guide.

It is hoped therefore that this guide will be a useful tool, assisting healthcare practitioners at all levels and in a variety of settings to recognise and acknowledge the requirements of their minority group patients, and to help them to develop and deliver appropriately sensitive services to those patients in their care.

Part 2 | The Faiths

Major world religions

Buddhism

Basic principles of the faith

Buddhism is a religion founded on the concept that people should be kind and considerate to each other, since good behaviour in this life will result in rebirth on a higher plane in the next. Buddhists believe that we should love and respect the whole of creation. Buddhists should not kill any living thing, and are expected to lead virtuous lives, avoiding stimulants such as drugs and alcohol. Self-discipline is recommended, as is open hospitality to those in need, and the giving of alms (in money or food) as a charitable deed. There is a structure of monks, who can be either men or, less commonly, women, who live simple lives and are supported wholly by the community.

Adherents to this faith follow the teachings of the Buddha, who was born in the 7th Century CE in the Nepal/northern Indian area, living there for some eighty years until his death. He lived simply, sharing his concepts with his followers, and concentrating on contemplation, wisdom and morality throughout his life.

The religious activities of his followers include prayers, chants, and the commitment to meditation and self-awareness. The aim of reincarnation and self-understanding is that the soul will eventually reach the highest place of consciousness, known as 'Nirvana'.

Diet

There are no religious dietary restrictions, although some Buddhists remain vegetarian, preferring to eat simply and not wishing to consume meat products. Some Buddhists will fast regularly as a form of self-denial.

Resulting restrictions

There are no evident restrictions resulting from diet, other than an awareness that vegetarian patients may wish to avoid medications with inappropriate constituent parts.

Notes about styles of dress, jewellery, hair

There are few restrictions. Monks will shave their heads and wear saffron-coloured robes; novice monks wear dark maroon robes.

Clinical interventions

The Buddhist patient recognises the sanctity of human life, and thus will accept clinical care. There are no particular interventions which are forbidden to them. Post-mortem organ donation may be accepted where it is the wish of the individual patient.

Contraception and abortion

There is no specific enjoinder against contraception and abortion, particularly if the mother's life is in danger, but it may be seen to contradict the fundamental wish to preserve and to value human life.

Matters surrounding birth

There are no particular restrictions relating to birth.

Matters surrounding death

Buddhists will wish to follow certain rituals at the time of death, which will vary according to the sect and school of the individuals concerned. Some Buddhists believe that the body should be left for 24 hours, during which time prayers are said, and candles left burning around the room. Appropriate religious leaders will attend the body at this time. Cremation is the preferred option.

Interpreters

There are no particular difficulties noted.

Religious festivals and observances

Buddhist festivals and holy days are governed by the lunar calendar, and the dates of the celebrations can vary according to the country of origin of the followers.

- **The Birthday of the Buddha** (Nirvana Day): 8 or 15 February (alternative dates) – nearest to the full moon in February.
- **Buddhist New Year**: three-day festival after the first full moon – the month of celebration varies from January to April according to the location and branch of Buddhism being followed.
- **Buddha Day** – commemoration of the Buddha's death (which for some followers also celebrates the Buddha's birth and enlightenment): the first full moon day in May.
- **Dharma Day** – the anniversary of the beginning of the Buddha's teachings: the first full moon in July.

Naming systems

The naming system is likely to relate to the patient's country of origin.

Christianity

Basic principles of the faith

Christianity is one of the major world religions, and is one of the three Abrahamic faiths (the others being Islam and Judaism). The Christian religion is over some two thousand years old, and was founded by the followers of Jesus Christ (Jesus of Nazareth). Christians believe that Jesus is the Son of God and Saviour of the World, conceived immaculately by the Virgin Mary – the Virgin Mary is a particularly significant figure in the Roman Catholic Church. Christianity is found in many forms throughout the world, including Roman Catholic, Protestant, Churches of England and Scotland, Greek Orthodox, and many other smaller faith branches (some of which are mentioned later in this text). Each branch is led by a different religious leader, e.g. the Church of England is led by the Archbishop of Canterbury, but the British monarch is titular head of the Church of England; the leader of the Roman Catholic

Christianity

Church is His Holiness the Pope. The holy book for all Christians is the Bible, which comprises the Old and New Testaments (the latter of which includes the Gospels).

Diet

There are few dietary restrictions, although historically fish was eaten on Fridays. Some Christians will fast during the period of Lent, leading up to Easter, but this is not a daylight fast, generally being abstention from certain stimulants or favourite foods, as self-discipline during this holy period.

Resulting restrictions

There are no evident restrictions resulting from diet, although some Christians may not wish to take alcohol-based medication during the Lenten period.

Notes about styles of dress, jewellery, hair

There are no restrictions, although certain Christian communities believe in covering the hair and wearing respectfully modest clothing when in Church or on holy sites as a visitor.

Clinical interventions

There are generally no restrictions relating to clinical interventions, although some sects (e.g. Jehovah's Witnesses, mentioned later in this guide, object to interventions involving the exchange of blood). Many Christians consider organ donation as an act of compassion and love to their fellow men, so will volunteer willingly.

Contraception and abortion

Some branches of the Christian faith (e.g. Roman Catholicism) believe that contraception goes against the word of the Bible, which states that human life is to be preserved, and therefore in certain parts of the world abortion is also banned. However, in other communities there is no specific enjoinder against contraception and abortion, particularly if the mother's life is in danger, but it may be seen to contradict the fundamental wish to preserve and to value human life. Certain medical practitioners are against abortion and will not counsel women patients about the process.

Matters surrounding birth

There are no particular restrictions relating to birth. A baby can be baptised into the faith (also known as Christening) at a very early stage after birth if its life is in danger.

Matters surrounding death

Christians may wish to be buried or cremated, and either is permitted, with either a church ceremony or a religious ceremony at a crematorium. Many Christians may wish to see a Christian chaplain, or their own religious minister, when death is approaching.

Interpreters

Christians live in many countries in the world, and thus interpretation for foreign nationals, for the language of their birth country, may be an occasional requirement.

Religious festivals and observances

Sunday is traditionally the day of rest, as described in Genesis in the Bible. **Easter week**, leading up to the day when Jesus was crucified and then rose again three days later, is significant in Biblical terms. The 40 day period before Easter is called **Lent**, when people may fast. The Sunday before Easter is **Palm Sunday**, when Jesus entered Jerusalem for the last time. **Maundy Thursday** commemorates the Last Supper where Jesus sat with his disciples; **Good Friday** commemorates the crucifixion and is significant in the calendar. **Easter Sunday** is the day when the tomb was found empty and Jesus rose from the dead.

Ascension Day is 40 days after Easter, when the Bible describes Jesus as ascending into Heaven and returning to God, the Father (from where Christians believe that he will return at a future time). Whitsunday is related to be the day when the Holy Spirit descended, 50 days after Easter. **Christmas Day** (December 25) celebrates the birth of Jesus in the stable in Bethlehem. Many Christians will attend church services weekly, and particularly on these occasions. There are in addition many saints' days in the Christian calendar.

Naming systems

The naming system is likely to relate to the patient's country of origin. Many Christians arrange for their children to be baptised by a priest or official from their branch of the faith, making promises to bring up their child in that faith and appointing Godparents to support this – this ceremony is known as Christening, but no specific name is added to the child's given name at this time. People who convert to Christianity in adulthood can be baptised at any age.

Hinduism

Basic principles of the faith

Hinduism is a religion based on the worship of many gods, each of whom serves a different purpose. Each of the gods is believed to be a different manifestation of a single superior Being. Hinduism permeates every aspect of its followers' lives – there is a considerable social and caste system inherent in this religion. Hindus believe in reincarnation, and a person's place in the caste system in this life is consequent upon his or her performance in a previous life. The caste system also determines a person's place in the social structure, and it is rare for people to mix across castes. The highest caste level is the Brahmins, who are the most devout and thus the most strict observers of their faith.

Prayer is a vital part of Hindu worship, and this takes place either in the home – every home is likely to have a shrine to their individual god(s) – or in the temple.

Diet

Hindus tend to be vegetarian, and some may not eat eggs. The cow is considered a sacred animal, and thus beef in any form is unacceptable. Alcohol and smoking are allowed, but not encouraged.

Resulting restrictions

There are no evident restrictions resulting from diet, other than an awareness that vegetarian patients may wish to avoid medication with inappropriate constituent parts, and anything containing beef extract (e.g. beef insulin for diabetic patients, beef gelatine in capsules) will be unacceptable.

Notes about styles of dress, jewellery, hair

Jewellery and religious accoutrements are important to Hindus, and they may prefer not to remove them for clinical examinations. This applies to both men and women. Brahmins may wear a sacred cord around the body, and will remove it only under extreme circumstances.

Married women are identifiable by a red dot (known as a bhindi) on their foreheads – this significant mark has now been adopted by some non-Hindus as a fashion statement. A married woman may also wear glass bangles on her arms. These must not be broken intentionally, because that should only be done deliberately after her husband's death.

Hindus exhort cleanliness, and, as with other religions originating in the East, they believe that it is unclean to sit in washing-water, so use a shower whenever possible. Both men and women dress modestly.

Clinical interventions

There are no restrictions regarding blood transfusions or organ donation, the latter is accepted as an integral part of the Hindu way of life, sustaining other life. Traditional medicines may be used alongside NHS interventions, and their use should be noted in case of possible interactions. Women may not wish to expose their entire body to healthcare professionals, and may prefer to be examined by a female doctor or nurse.

Contraception and abortion

There are no specific instructions about contraception.

Hinduism

Matters surrounding birth

At birth, a holy Hindu symbol is written inside the baby's mouth, using a sweet liquid. Women prefer to remain at home for 40 days following the birth.

Matters surrounding death

Traditionally and in their homelands, deceased Hindus will be cremated on a funeral pyre, and the ashes scattered into running water. In the United Kingdom, cremation is the preferred option; if they were not born in the UK, families may wish to return their deceased's ashes to their original homeland. Post-mortems are disliked.

Interpreters

Members of the elderly immigrant population may speak little or no English, but there are no particular difficulties noted.

Religious festivals and observances

The principal holy days for Hindus are:

- significant birthdays of their gods, which occur throughout the year;
- **Diwali**, the Festival of Light, when candles are lit – this occurs in the late autumn.

Their religious calendar is based on the lunar cycle, so the exact dates will vary from year to year. Every 12 years, the **Kumbh Mela** festival takes place in northern India. Millions of devout Hindus travel from all over the world to the River Ganges to bathe, at a time in the religious calendar when it is considered that this ablution will absolve them of their sins.

Naming systems

The naming system is likely to relate to the patient's country of origin.

Islam

Basic principles of the faith

The translation of the word 'Islam' from the Arabic is 'submission', that is, submission to the will of God. People who follow the Islamic faith are known as Muslims (also spelled occasionally as Moslems, or archaically known as Mohammedans), and they refer to God as 'Allah'. Islam is one of the three Abrahamic faiths, the others being Christianity and Judaism. All three acknowledge the importance of the prophet Abraham (known to Muslims as Ibrahim). The Abrahamic faiths share many aspects, and equally differ in many ways. Many of the Old Testament prophets and stories are common to all three religions.

Many non-Muslims are surprised to learn that Muslims believe in Jesus (who they call Isa). They acknowledge Jesus as a prophet alongside others, and they believe that there was another prophet who followed him, who was Mohammed. The prophet Mohammed was an ordinary man, who in his fortieth year received messages through the Angel Gabriel (Jibreel), who subsequently dictated to him the holy book which Muslims follow as the word of Allah, known as the Koran (Qu'ran).

Mohammed lived during the 7th Century CE in the two cities of Mecca and Medina (which are now in the modern kingdom of Saudi Arabia). These cities are the first and second holiest places in Islam. Every Muslim who has the capability and resources to do so must visit Mecca at least once in his or her lifetime, to perform the annual pilgrimage, the Hajj. In order to contain numbers attending the pilgrimage, Hajj visas are now issued to enter Saudi Arabia at that time, and numbers are restricted from individual countries across the world. Currently, some three million people attend Hajj every year.

The dates for Hajj to take place, and for fasting in the month of Ramadan, are determined by the Muslim calendar, which is based on the phases of the moon, and thus runs on different intervals to the Julian calendar also used worldwide (the latter being the twelve months from January to December each year).

Islam

The majority of Muslim patients will observe the five pillars of their faith, which are:

- to make the declaration of faith, confirming that they believe that there is only one God, and that Mohammed is his Prophet or Messenger;
- to perform Hajj at least once in their lifetime, if they have the means to do so;
- to perform the five daily prayers (Salat) at the set times;
- to give to charity (this obligation is known as Zakat);
- to fast during the lunar month of Ramadan.

The faith is based on principles of modesty, decency, cleanliness, and brotherhood. The family unit is very important, and it is relatively unusual for a Muslim, male or female, to remain unmarried. Arranged marriage, with the participants' consent, is frequently the norm. Sexual contact between persons who are not married is unacceptable.

Diet

Muslims are forbidden to eat pork and any pork products. They are not permitted to drink alcohol or to eat or drink any products containing alcohol. Some Muslims will not eat shellfish. Meat products must be 'halal', which means that the animal or bird has been killed in the name of Allah, and that the meat contains no blood when prepared for consumption.

During the holy month of Ramadan, the majority of compliant Muslims will neither eat nor drink between the hours of sunrise and sunset (but will do so during the hours of darkness). Many will not take any medication during the hours of the fast.

Resulting restrictions

Healthcare professionals must be aware that their Muslim patients cannot take medication with either a porcine or an alcohol base; for example, therefore, care must be taken in prescribing insulin. Capsules prepared with gelatin casings may also be unacceptable.

Fasting is very important, and must be allowed for. If a patient is too ill to fast, they are exempted, as are pregnant or menstruating women, the elderly, and pre-pubescent children – but many will wish to participate anyway, or make up the days later in the year.

Modesty is very important. Muslims are exhorted not to display their naked bodies, or parts of their bodies, before anyone except their marriage partners. If this must happen, consent must be sought. Most will consent to examination on clinical grounds, although many may prefer to be examined by someone of their own gender.

Notes about styles of dress, jewellery, hair

Muslims are enjoined to dress modestly. For men, this means not displaying the area between the waist and the knees; for women, only the face, hands and feet should be visible. There are many cultural variations to this: strict Arab women will cover their everyday clothing from head to foot in black robes when they leave the house, and Afghan women may cover completely in an all-enveloping burka. In other cultures, Muslim women may wear a headscarf (hijab) with their normal modest clothing, and in the UK many employers have now introduced a suitable hijab into their company uniforms. Many black African women will wear a colourful turban to conceal their hair, which complements their flowing dresses.

Many Muslim men wear a beard. Other than male facial hair, bodily hair is deemed to be unhygienic, and both men and women may regularly remove all of it.

Healthcare professionals should be aware that some Muslims prefer to use separate towels for drying the upper and lower parts of the body. When undertaking clinical examinations, the healthcare professional's hands should always be washed before moving elsewhere on the patient's body, and separate towels used where possible.

Clinical interventions

Generally speaking, the Muslim patient will welcome clinical interventions; Islam encourages its followers to look after their bodily health as well as their spiritual wellbeing.

Blood transfusions are generally acceptable. Organ donation may not be so; in particular, interventions such as heart valve surgery may not be acceptable where the replacement valve is constructed from pig's tissue. In 1995 the Muslim Law (Shariah) Council UK issued a religious opinion that, in general, Muslims may carry donor cards if that is their personal preference; the next of kin may give permission for post-mortem organ donations; and the Council supported organ donation as a general principle towards saving the life of another person. This view may not be generally shared, and therefore individual decisions must be made in individual cases.

Contraception and abortion

Some Muslim patients will accept contraception, others will not. Abortion is not liked, but may be accepted on clinical grounds if there is risk to the mother.

Matters surrounding birth

Language difficulties have sometimes prevented pregnant immigrant Muslim women accessing antenatal care. With adequate interpretation facilities and the production of information leaflets in several languages for local communities, this should be less common.

The first words which a newborn baby hears are from the Koran. Male babies will be circumcised within a few days of birth. The practice of female circumcision, which is still undertaken in certain parts of the world, is not an Islamic practice but originates in local culture.

Matters surrounding death

Ideally, the terminally-ill Muslim patient will wish to die at home, surrounded by his family. They will wish to hear words from the Koran read; Koranic texts are the first words heard by a new-born baby, and should be the last as the dying person departs this world.

The dead body should only be handled by fellow Muslims. The body must be washed and shrouded (ideally in the robes which the person wore when they completed the Hajj, if they have done so). The washing should be undertaken by persons of the same gender as the deceased.

Muslims bury their dead, facing the direction of Mecca (south-east from the UK), ideally within 24 hours of death. Post-mortems are not liked because of the resultant delay in burial, but are usually tolerated on clinical grounds.

Some Muslim families may wish to repatriate their dead to their homelands, in which case early certification of death may be requested, in order to enable this to happen within the tight timescale desired.

Interpreters

Many Muslims in the UK are either from second- or third-generation families, and many are converts from the indigenous population, so language problems should not arise for these groups. There are still however a large number of people whose English is limited or non-existent (particularly the elderly). Traditionally, their children or marriage partners have interpreted for them during clinical consultations; this is not an ideal situation, and can lead to prejudices and misunderstandings, so an impartial interpreter may be preferable.

Religious festivals and observances

Muslims celebrate several holy days, the principal of which are:

- **Eid ul-Fitr**, which happens at the end of **Ramadan**
- **Eid ul-Adha**, which takes place during the time of the **Hajj**, and reminds them of those undertaking the pilgrimage.

The dates of these events come forward by approximately 10 days every year, in line with the changing phases of the moon in the lunar calendar. Different sects of Islam also celebrate other significant dates in the Muslim calendar.

The Muslim holiday day, in all branches of the faith, is Friday, when the midday prayers are important.

Naming systems

The majority of Muslims will have a personal name and a religious name, e.g. Mohammed (the personal name) and Ali (the religious name). A family may not have a common surname – potentially, all members of one branch of a family may have different names, although it is becoming more common that the children of a family take the name of the father. Historically, married women have tended

Islam

to retain their own names. In the same way that the Scottish 'Mac' indicates 'son of', the prefix 'bin' or 'ibn' indicates 'son of' in Muslim society.

Since the majority of Muslim patients will have a name directly related to their religion, it is often impossible to gauge their nationality from their name. Converts to Islam may often adopt a Muslim name, which is likely to be Arabic in origin. It is therefore important to ask a Muslim patient how they would like to be addressed.

Other useful information

Muslims follow strict rules about the use of the left and right hands for certain functions. The left hand is used for washing the body after visits to the toilet, and is therefore 'unclean'; as a result, only the right hand is used for eating. They prefer to wash in running water or a shower, as the practice of sitting in dirty water during a bath is considered unclean.

After using the toilet, some Muslim patients may prefer to wash their bodies with water, instead of using toilet paper. A jug of water, provided exclusively for this purpose, will be appreciated.

Judaism

Judaism

Basic principles of the faith

The Judaic religion is another of the three Abrahamic faiths, the others being Christianity and Islam. All three acknowledge the importance of the prophet Abraham. The Abrahamic faiths share many aspects, and equally differ in many ways. Many of the Old Testament prophets and stories are common to all three religions.

The holy book of the Jews is called the Torah, which comprises the first five books of the Christian Bible, and their code of conduct is called the Talmud. Their religious leaders are known as rabbis. Judaism affects all aspects of daily life. The most important aspects of the Torah relate to the Ten Commandments, received by Moses directly from God.

Jews in the United Kingdom are a relatively small but significant and well-established community, spread throughout the country. They follow their religion in differing ways, depending upon the sects or branches to which they belong. Orthodox Jews are the most strict in their religious observances. Like other religions, their behaviour is based on principles of modesty, decency, cleanliness and brotherhood. The family unit is very important. Hassidic Jews form quite a closed community, and may not mix readily with people outside their sect.

Judaism

Diet

Jews are forbidden to eat pork and any pork products, and shellfish. Some Jews are not permitted to drink alcohol or any products containing alcohol. Meat products must be 'kosher', which means that the animal has been killed according to Jewish tradition. Orthodox Jews will not eat meat and milk together, and use separate dishes and utensils for these food groups.

Jews will fast annually on the Day of Atonement 'Yom Kippur', and may do so at other times throughout the year. Some Jews may choose to eat only cold food on a Saturday, which is their Sabbath, as on that day they are prohibited from working or carrying out strenuous activities after sunset on Friday – which can be said to include preparing meals. For Orthodox Jews, these prohibitions may also include activities such as switching on an electric light, or answering the telephone. Dietary restrictions can also apply during the holy week of Passover ('Pesach'), which occurs in the first quarter of the year – during this week, restrictions may apply to yeast products such as bread, cakes, and certain medications. Wine may also be replaced with unfermented wine during Passover.

Resulting restrictions

Healthcare professionals must be aware that their Jewish patients may not wish to take medication with a porcine base; for example, care must be taken in prescribing insulin and gelatin-based capsules. However, since the protection of life is an important aspect of their faith, this can be waived, and porcine vaccines and other medication may be acceptable – it is important to ask the patient. The local rabbi

Judaism

will usually be willing to discuss individual medications, and to advise which items are considered to be 'kosher', and therefore acceptable to Jewish patients.

If patients are fasting, they will not wish to take oral medication, but will accept it by other routes. Personal modesty is important. Orthodox Jews will prefer clinical examinations to be undertaken by someone of the same gender.

Notes about styles of dress, jewellery, hair

Jews dress modestly. Examples of particular requirements are:

• Orthodox Jewesses are likely to cover their hair with a wig, which is only removed in private;
• Hassidic Jewish men wear their hair long in ringlets ('peyot') at the front, dress formally, and always wear a hat, even indoors, when away from home;
• Jewish men may frequently wear a skullcap ('yarmulke'), which is always worn when in the synagogue.

Clinical interventions

The Jewish patient recognises the sanctity of human life, and thus will accept clinical care and certain interventions. Blood transfusions are acceptable, although organ donations may not be liked as there may be objections to interfering with the body of the deceased after death; however, the principle of organ donation to save the lives of others is widespread. Interventions such as heart valve surgery may not be acceptable where the replacement valve is constructed from pig's tissue.

Contraception and abortion

Some Jewish patients will accept contraception, particularly if the mother's health is otherwise at risk. Abortion is not liked, but may be accepted on clinical grounds.

Matters surrounding birth

There are no particular restrictions relating to birth. Male babies will be circumcised, usually on the eighth day after birth. Traditionally, this duty is undertaken by a holy man known as a 'mohel'. Haemophiliac boys do not have to be circumcised, but are still considered to be Jewish without their having undergone this otherwise essential operation. The right to be Jewish is conferred down the maternal line.

Matters surrounding death

Jewish people will be buried, preferably within 24 hours of death. The body is wrapped in a plain sheet, and someone remains with the body at all times until burial. Cremation is forbidden by Jewish law, but may be acceptable to some. Post-mortems will be discouraged unless required by the law of the land.

After the funeral, the immediate family remain at home and 'sit shivah' for seven days, being visited and brought food by relatives and friends during the mourning period, and refraining from daily activities.

Interpreters

There is a resident Jewish population in the UK for whom English is their mother tongue. Some elderly immigrant Jews may only speak Yiddish; Hebrew is the language of prayers and of more modern-day Jews. Immigrant Jews may also speak the language of their mother country. Some interpretation facilities may be required.

Religious festivals and observances

The principal holy days for Jews are:

- the Sabbath ('**Shabbat**') – every Saturday – from sunset on Friday until sunset on Saturday
- the Jewish New Year '**Rosh Hashanah**'
- '**Yom Kippur**' – 24 hours of fasting
- **Passover** – in the Spring, celebrating the Exodus into Egypt
- Harvest Festival '**Shavuot**'
- Feast of Tabernacles '**Sukkot**'
- '**Hanukkah**' – an eight-day festival in December, when candles are lit
- '**Purim**', which celebrates the story of Esther

The religious calendar is based on the lunar cycle, so the exact dates of these holy days and festivals will vary from year to year.

Naming systems

The majority of Jews will have names relating to their religion. The family name structure is familial, in that wives and children take the family name of their husband and father. The word 'ben' as part of a family name is used to indicate 'son of', as in, e.g. 'David ben Gurion'.

Other useful information

The traditional Jewish diet may be high in carbohydrates, and nutrition may be inadequate.

Tay-Sachs disease has been noted as being prevalent in certain Jewish sects; this is a genetic condition of childhood, which almost always leads to death in infancy.

Paganism

Basic principles of the faith

Paganism is one of the oldest religions, with the belief in Mother Earth as the provider of everything, and as the main object of worship. Pagans believe in the equality of all creation. Paganism can be found in different forms, but the central tenets are the same in the majority of them.

Since this religion can be perceived as unusual, and in some instances might appear sinister to the uninformed, Pagans may be reluctant to identify themselves unless absolutely necessary, for fear of prejudice.

Diet

Many Pagans follow vegetarian or vegan diets, to confirm their unity with the world and all its living things. They will be reluctant to kill deliberately for food, since all creatures are seen as equal and are to be respected as such.

Clinical interventions

There are no particular restrictions regarding clinical or surgical interventions.

Matters surrounding birth

There are no particular birth rituals, other than general celebration of the event.

Matters surrounding death

Death is a significant rite of passage, since the soul is returning to Mother Earth. It will be important to ask the patient or family members exactly what they would like to do, both before and after death. Green burials may be a preference.

Paganism

Rastafarianism

Rastafarianism

Basic principles of the faith

Rastafarianism is a social movement which established itself in Jamaica in the early 1930s. Its values combine philosophical tenets and the religious belief in a black God and Messiah. They do not, however, consider themselves as Christians.

Since Jamaica was colonised in the 17th century CE, the expression of religious belief has been one way of demonstrating resistance to oppression. Rastafarian culture combines all aspects of the slave culture and the ethics of the freedom fighters.

The one-time Emperor of Ethiopia, Haile Selassie I (1892-1975) is a core figure in the religion. Rastafarians believe Haile Selassie is God (Jah Rastafari), and that he will return to Africa (or more specifically, to Ethiopia) to repatriate those members of the black community who are living in exile. The name 'Rastafarianism' is taken from 'Ras', meaning 'prince', and 'Tafari', the name of the Emperor of Ethiopia, where many of the African slaves originated.

At Rastafarian prayer gatherings, 'ganja' (marijuana) is smoked communally in a water-pipe; it is considered a holy weed.

Diet

In common with some other religions, Rastafarians will not eat shellfish or pork, or their derivatives.

Rastafarianism

Resulting restrictions

Any medication containing pork derivatives, e.g. porcine insulin, or gelatin-based capsules, will be unacceptable. Interventions such as heart valve surgery may not be acceptable where the replacement valve is constructed from pig's tissue.

Notes about styles of dress, jewellery, hair

Many Rastafarian women dress modestly. Rastafarian men are conspicuous by their dreadlocks or long matted hair, which may be covered with a beret-type hat. The hairstyle is an important symbol of their beliefs, and should not be cut or trimmed without the patient's permission. Clothing often reflects the Rasta colours of red, green and gold.

Clinical interventions

Organ transplants and blood transfusions are not generally liked (see also Resulting Restrictions, above).

Contraception and abortion

Traditionally, Rastafarians do not practice contraception.

Matters surrounding birth

There are no particular issues surrounding birth.

Matters surrounding death

It is likely that Rastafarians will visit a dying member of their community, and may wish to pray with them. Burial is preferred.

Interpreters

The Jamaican patois can be no more difficult to understand than any other dialect in the UK. Visitors to this country may be accompanied by a local resident, if interpretation is likely to be a problem.

Religious festivals and observance

All-night celebrations can be held to mark special occasions throughout the year, such as the commemoration of the emancipation from slavery, and on significant dates in the life of Haile Selassie (see above).

Naming systems

The naming system is the same as that generally encountered in the indigenous population of the UK, with a personal and family name being used.

Many people from the Caribbean will have family names which historically relate back to the slave days, in that, for instance, a slave owner named McKay would give his surname to the children born to his slaves. That family name is likely to have carried on down through the generations into the present day.

Sikhism

Basic principles of the faith

The Sikh faith developed from Hinduism in the late 16th Century CE. Whereas Hindus worship many gods, Sikhs worship only one. They share many common aspects with Hindus, in particular a belief in rebirth. Their temple is known as a 'Gurdwara'. The majority of Sikhs originated in the north-west of the Indian subcontinent.

Diet

Sikhs tend to be vegetarian, although they are permitted to eat meat when the animal has been slaughtered with a single stroke. 'Halal' (Muslim) and 'Kosher' (Jewish) meat is forbidden to Sikhs, although their animals are also killed in accordance with their religious beliefs. Beef may be avoided, out of respect for Hindus. Pork is also considered unclean, out of deference to Muslims. Alcohol is discouraged, but may be taken. Smoking is forbidden.

Resulting restrictions

Healthcare professionals must be aware that vegetarian patients may wish to avoid medication with inappropriate constituent parts. Medicines containing beef or pork (e.g. beef or pork insulin for diabetic patients), and capsules containing gelatin, may be unacceptable.

Sikhism

Notes about styles of dress, jewellery, hair

Sikh men are obliged by their religion to wear the five signs of Sikhism, sometimes called 'the five Ks', namely:

- 'kesh' – uncut hair worn in a bun, covered with a turban
- 'kangha' – a comb
- 'kara' – a steel bangle
- 'kirpan' – a symbolic dagger
- 'kaccha' – symbolic shorts (worn as underwear).

They will be very reluctant to remove any of these symbols, for any reason.

Sikh women wear their hair long, covered with a light scarf ('dupatta'). They tend to wear the traditional 'salwar kameez' (lightweight dress and trousers) from their homeland. Wedding jewellery is extremely important to married women. Both men and women dress modestly.

As with other Eastern religions, Sikhs believe that it is unclean to sit in washing-water, so use a shower whenever possible, to clean their bodies.

Clinical interventions

Blood transfusions and organ transplants are permitted, although heart valve transplants constructed from pig's tissue should be discussed with the patient beforehand. The Sikh philosophy places emphasis on the importance of giving, and putting others before oneself, and performing noble deeds. Since the human body is not needed in the next life, organ donation is felt to be consistent with the spirit of Sikh teachings.

Traditional medicines may be used alongside NHS medication, and their use should be declared to the healthcare professional, and noted in the patient's clinical records in case of any possible interactions. Women may prefer to be examined by a female doctor or nurse.

Contraception and abortion

There are no specific prohibitions about contraception, although large families are considered desirable. Abortion is allowed in extreme circumstances.

Matters surrounding birth

There are no significant requirements surrounding birth, although women may prefer to remain at home for 40 days following the birth.

Matters surrounding death

Sikh families will wish to deal with all the death rituals of their family members. Non-Sikhs are allowed to attend the body, but the family must be consulted. The body will be cremated within 24 hours of death, and the ashes scattered in running water. Post-mortems are allowed when necessary.

Interpreters

Members of the elderly immigrant population may speak little or no English, but there are no particular difficulties noted.

Religious festivals and observances

The principal holy days for Sikhs include:

- 'Vaisakhi', the Sikh New Year
- 'Diwali', the Festival of Light, when candles are lit
- birthdays and death anniversaries of principal figures in the faith.

The religious calendar is based on the lunar cycle, so the exact dates will vary from year to year. The Sikh holy day is Sunday.

Naming systems

It is important for healthcare personnel to understand the naming system in Sikh families. Sikh names have three parts. The first name is personal, the second is religious, and the third is their family name. The religious name rarely varies, and is likely to be 'Singh' meaning a lion, for men, and 'Kaur', meaning 'princess' for a woman.

The family (third) name may not always be used in daily life. For example, a man's name may be (first name) Singh, or (first name) Singh (third name) – this will be the same person and both are correct, so it is vital for the patient's medical records that consistency is used in recording these names for Sikh patients.

Christian sects and other faith groups

Chapter 4

Jehovah's Witnesses

Basic principles of the faith

The Jehovah's Witnesses are Christian people, who live strictly by the teachings of the Bible. They have great respect for the sanctity of life. They believe that Jesus is the Son of God, but they do not recognise the Trinity. They use no religious symbols in worship, and believe that living a truthful life, loving one's fellow man, and demonstrating genuine love for their Maker encompass true worship. They remain neutral in hostility, yet respect authority, and do not interfere in national politics.

Jehovah's Witnesses will mix freely in society, although they may not share in all recreational activities. They are probably best-known outside the faith for their practice of spreading the word of God, though door-to-door calling, and distributing the Watchtower publication, since they see these activities as their Biblical duty.

Diet

Following Biblical interpretation, Jehovah's Witnesses will not consume anything containing blood or blood products. They also believe that the Bible prohibits the use of tobacco and addictive drugs. Alcohol is permitted, in moderation.

Resulting restrictions

The principal prohibition, arising from the Bible's instruction not to 'consume' blood, is that Jehovah's Witnesses often refuse blood

Jehovah's Witnesses

transfusions. However, there is considerable discussion as to whether non-blood alternatives are acceptable, and fractions of blood may be given if acceptable to the patient. Personal choice in this matter is allowed.

It must be remembered that it is the receipt of blood which is at issue; it may be acceptable to the patient for blood to be taken for pathological analysis.

Otherwise, all clinical care is sought, and advice will be followed.

Hospital Liaison Committee

Jehovah's Witnesses have access to a Hospital Liaison Committee, who will negotiate with medical and nursing staff on behalf of these patients regarding appropriate treatments involving blood and blood products. Individuals carry a small card bearing details of how the Committee can be contacted. This Committee is part of an international network, and is recognised and respected by the major institutions. The Committee will provide information for healthcare professionals about the Jehovah's Witnesses' views on receiving blood and blood products. It is also instrumental in making this information available to everyone through various internet websites.

Notes about styles of dress, jewellery, hair

There are no particular dress habits other than modest everyday clothing appropriate to the country of origin.

Clinical interventions

As stated above, blood transfusions or whole blood may be unacceptable. Individuals may decide whether or not to receive organ transplants. The extension of life by mechanical means may not be acceptable. There are no prohibitions against receiving immunisations and vaccinations.

Contraception and abortion

Contraception is permitted, abortion is not. The sanctity of life once begun must be respected.

Matters surrounding birth

There are no particular issues surrounding birth.

Matters surrounding death

Jehovah's Witnesses will wish to die naturally, and may wish to see an Elder from their community at this time. Post-mortems are acceptable, and are by personal decision. The patient's wishes may have been known in advance, and should be respected.

Interpreters

In the UK, Jehovah's Witnesses are likely to be English-speaking, or, if visiting from outside the UK, they will bring an English-speaking member of their community with them to any clinical consultation.

Religious festivals and observances

Jehovah's Witnesses do not celebrate Christian or national holidays. They will celebrate weddings and anniversaries with parties. Their only religious commemoration is that of the Memorial of Christ's Death.

Naming systems

This will follow that of their country of origin.

Other useful information

Jehovah's Witnesses lead morally upright lives, believing in monogamous marriage for life, with no sexual contact outside that relationship. They therefore believe that they may be protected from sexually transmitted diseases. Likewise, they believe that their standards of personal cleanliness may render them less likely to contract infections arising from poor hygiene habits.

Jehovah's
Witnesses

Mormons

The Mormons are Christians, also known as members of the Church of the Latter-Day Saints. Their origins and main base are in Utah, in the United States of America.

Mormons follow a strict moral code. Alcohol, cigarettes, and other stimulants are prohibited to them. At one time, it was acceptable for a Mormon man to have several wives and many children, and although this practice is known to continue on occasion in outlying areas, it has been prohibited for some years.

By leading a pure life, it is possible to attain the highest level of priesthood within their Church. Mormons attaining this honour will wear a ritual undergarment, which should be respected and only removed when absolutely necessary. Outer dress is otherwise modest.

Plymouth Brethren

The Plymouth Brethren are Christians, originating in Britain in the early part of the nineteenth century. They prefer simple Bible study, and their gatherings are similar to those held in Old Testament times, with hymn-singing and gospel readings. Prayers are said by the male members of the community, and they partake of bread and wine.

They are peace-loving people, and many of the original Brethren may have been conscientious objectors to military service.

Some Plymouth Brethren belong to 'exclusive' sects; this means that they like to keep themselves apart from other people. These people may wish to eat apart; they do not use personal computers, or listen to the radio, watch television, or read the popular press. Any such wishes should be respected. Objections to the use of computer technology during clinical consultations have not been identified.

Clothing is modest, and many women prefer to cover their hair with a scarf or hat.

Female patients may prefer to be examined by a female healthcare professional.

There are no restrictions applying to blood transfusions, organ transplants, or immunisations and vaccinations.

The Bruderhof Community

The Bruderhof are a Christian group, with several centres in the United States of America, and communities at a number of locations in the UK, Germany and Australia. The basis of their faith is to follow Jesus' teachings of the Sermon on the Mount, of non-violence, brotherly love, and sexual purity. They are tolerant of other faith communities.

Marriage is viewed as a unique, life-long commitment. The elderly in their communities are revered. Individuals dedicate themselves to the community for life, although young people growing up are encouraged to see life for themselves in the outside world before making their own commitment (there are parallels in this practice with the Amish communities in the United States of America). The Bruderhof believe that their common way of life provides a solution to all issues, whether political, economic or social, and they actively support the underprivileged.

They are frank people, believing that gossip is undesirable and that direct and honest address maintains open relationships, encouraging friendships, since no grievances are then held.

Members of the community dress modestly. The women's clothing is distinctive, often comprising a loose-fitting pinafore dress and a small headscarf worn tied at the back beneath the hairline.

In the United States, the Bruderhof run their own schools and day care centres; in the UK, they will join mainstream schooling.

Members of the community will actively seek medical advice in time of need.

The Bruderhof lead morally upright lives, believing in monogamous marriage for life, with no sexual contact outside that relationship. This may lead to a perception that they may be protected from sexually transmitted diseases, and cervical cancers.

Female patients may prefer to be examined by a female healthcare practitioner.

Other significant groups

Chapter 5

The Chinese population, and Chinese medicine

Chinese people have been resident in the UK for many years, many of them having come to this country to work in the family restaurant trade. They are to be found throughout this country, and although they have integrated into mainstream life, they may often still maintain the ways of their country of origin in their own family and social groups.

The religion followed by the majority of Chinese is Buddhism, in several of its forms; Christianity is also followed in lesser numbers.

The Chinese naming system usually shows the family name first, followed by personal names, although in the UK many Chinese have now adopted the local style of personal name/family name. It is important to check the name, to ensure that the family name and personal name are shown on medical records in the correct order. Many women follow the norm in Eastern countries of retaining their own family name when they marry.

The Chinese calendar is complex, with the months based on a lunar and solar cycle. In order to catch up with the solar cycle, a month is added every seven years in a nineteen-year cycle. It is for this reason that the Chinese New Year falls on a different date every year.

The Chinese New Year is a long festival, commencing with the first new moon of their New Year, and ending when that moon is full. The celebrations are family events, with street processions and feasts taking place; domestically, great emphasis is placed on cleaning the house, to sweep out the old year.

Chinese

Many Chinese people use traditional Chinese medicines, and practitioners can be found in many towns and cities. The use of traditional Chinese medicines is now also becoming increasingly popular in some areas amongst the indigenous population. The principle behind the practice of Chinese medicine is that healthiness is subject to opposing forces within the body, which must be balanced in order to maintain good health. The use of acupuncture and appropriate medicinal treatment can release blockages in the flow of vital energy, and thus restore balance to the body.

As with other forms of natural medicine, it is important to ascertain whether alternative medicines are being taken when prescribing for individuals, in case of interactions or contra-indications when taken with conventional prescription medication. Strict adherence to quantities and proportions of ingredients are very important, as some of the substances used can be toxic when administered incorrectly. Healthcare professionals should note that the Medicines Control Agency in the recent past has expressed considerable concerns about the regulation of the quality of products used in the formulation of Chinese medicines, and they recommend that patients should ensure that a clear list of ingredients, written in English, is shown on the packaging of the products. Prosecutions have taken place in the past where the ingredients have been illegally imported into the UK, or are of low quality, thus presenting a potential risk to overall health.

Roma, gypsies and travellers

The Roma (Romany people), gypsies and travellers

The travelling population is known by many names in different parts of the world. Their origins are very ancient, certainly stemming from as early as the Middle Ages. It is possible that the name 'gypsy' arose from a rumour that they came from Egypt, but it seems more likely that their origins were in northern India around the 10th century CE. The language which is common to the majority of these peoples (known as 'Romanes') certainly contains words which have similarities both to Indian sub-continental tongues and to Arabic.

The Roma's first recorded contact with Europeans was in the 14th century CE. They travelled to, and remained within, many European countries, including Germany and the Czech Republic, and the Irish travellers (many of whom can be found within the UK to this day) have their origins amongst these peoples.

There is an extensive clan system which embraces all Roma families. The family unit is very important, and there is a highly-defined social structure. Many Roma travel for most of the year but remain camped in one place over the winter months. They recognise the significance of interaction with non-Romanies, but intermarriage is not encouraged.

Since the Roma are used to a travelling lifestyle, there may be considerable reluctance to attend for medical treatment, and a stay in hospital may be treated with great suspicion. If a female Roma patient consents to examination, a female healthcare practitioner will be desirable to undertake this. The Roma may find it difficult to comply with the system of appointments for medical treatment, preferring to turn up when they are willing to accept clinical interventions. Call and recall systems will probably not be practical, since the patients are likely to have moved on. Notwithstanding these problems in integrating them into the healthcare system, the Roma people say that their way of life has enabled them to survive through great hardships and plagues, over the centuries.

Self-diagnosis and treatment, or reference to a wise woman within their communities, are the preferred methods of healthcare. The Roma people make extensive use of herbal and alternative medicines. Rituals and traditions are very important to them, and certain objects, people and creatures are believed to be tainted. There is a strong belief in 'bad luck', and any such portents will be avoided.

Despite their wandering lifestyle, cleanliness and personal hygiene are held to be important, and substances such as menstrual fluids are held to be unclean. The travelling lifestyle does however bring its own problems. Access to healthcare can be difficult, as the patient has no fixed address. If they do stay in any place for a time, access to primary care services can be unsatisfactory, since these patients may

Roma, gypsies and travellers

move on before diagnosis, or during a planned course of treatment. This moving on may be voluntary or by choice of others, if their family decides to leave the area.

Literacy, and the ability therefore to read and comprehend the written word, may also present a problem in this group of patients. It is believed that a large proportion of the adult travelling population may be illiterate. Children's schooling is patchy, where they can access school places, and is often fragmented by moving on.

Pregnant women rarely access antenatal care, and this may cause problems. Many women subsequently find that their clinical condition – or that of their unborn child – is such that, due to their lack of antenatal checks, they have to undergo Caesarean deliveries, which would not be their method of choice. The women traditionally prefer that childbirth is natural, and managed by other women within the family.

It is reported that traveller children are more frequently injured as a result of road accidents than the static population, since they are more exposed to the hazards of traffic. In the case of accident, travellers will often report direct to a local A&E facility.

The travelling population in general has a high incidence of respiratory disease.

There is also a high incidence of congenital abnormalities in some communities. Much of this may be attributed to travelling families' preference for intermarrying within the clan; similar circumstances have been noted amongst families from the Indian subcontinent, where spouses are sought within the wider family group.

The Irish travelling population (sometimes referred to as 'tinkers') has the same ancestral origins as the groups found elsewhere throughout Europe, and European Roma can be found as a distinct group in Ireland. Both Irish and European travellers will be found at sites located throughout the UK. They are an ancient people, and remain considerably disadvantaged on all fronts in all aspects of society.

References

Admani, K. (1993) in Hopkins, A. and Bahl, V. (eds), *Access to Health Care for People from Black and Ethnic Minorities,* London: Royal College of Physicians.

Ahmad, W.I.U. and Atkin, K. (eds) (1996) *'Race' and Community Care,* Buckingham: Open University Press.

Ahmed, T. (1998) 'The Asian experience' in Rawaf, S. and Bahl, V. (eds), *Assessing Health Needs of People from Ethnic Minority Groups,* London: Royal College of Physicians and the Faculty of Public Health Medicine.

Anon. (1996) 'UK's Muslim Law Council approves organ transplants' *Journal of Medical Ethics,* April; 22(2): 99. http://www.ncbi.nlm.nih.gov/pmc/articles/PMC1376922/pdf/jmedeth00301-0037.pdf (website accessed 7 August 2011).

Bahl, V. (1993) 'Ethnic minority groups – national perspective' in Hopkins, A. and Bahl, V. (eds), *Access to Health Care for People from Black and Ethnic Minorities,* London: Royal College of Physicians.

Balarajan, R. and Raleigh V.S. (1993) *The Health of the Nation: ethnicity and health, a guide for the NHS,* London: DoH.

Chapple, J. and Anionwu, E. (1998) 'Genetic services' in Rawaf, S. and Bahl, V. (eds), *Assessing Health Needs of People from Ethnic Minority Groups,* London: Royal College of Physicians and the Faculty of Public Health Medicine.

Cohen, R. (1994) *Frontiers of Identity: the British and the Others,* London: Longman Group Ltd.

Conference notes (2000) *Promoting Race Equality in Rural Areas conference,* Derby, 10 July 2000.

Connecting for Health (2011) Electronic Summary Care Record (ESCR) http://www.connectingforhealth.nhs.uk/systemsandservices/scr/documents/scrscope.pdf (accessed 8 March 2011).

Constantinides, P. (1977) 'The Greek Cypriots: Factors in the maintenance of ethnic identity' in Watson, J.L. (ed.), *Between Two Cultures: Migrants and Minorities in Britain,* Oxford: Blackwell Publishers.

Department of Health (1991) *The Patient's Charter,* London: DoH.

Department of Health (1996) *The Patient's Charter and You,* London: DoH.

Department of Health (2008a) *High Quality Care for All: NHS Next Stage Review* (The 'Darzi Report'), Norwich: The Stationery Office; website accessed 20 March 2011: http://www.dh.gov.uk/prod_consum_dh/groups/dh_digitalassets/@dh/@en/documents/digitalasset/dh_085828.pdf

Department of Health (2008b) *A High Quality Workforce: NHS Next Stage Review,* London: DoH; website accessed 20 March 2011: http://www.dh.gov.uk/prod_consum_dh/groups/dh_digitalassets/@dh/@en/documents/digitalasset/dh_085841.pdf

Department of Health Equality and Human Rights Group (2009): *Religion or Belief: A practical guide for the NHS,* London: Department of Health; website accessed 18 March 2011: http://www.dh.gov.uk/publications

Department of Health (2010) *The NHS Constitution (for England),* website accessed 19 March 2011: http://www.dh.gov.uk/prod_consum_dh/groups/dh_digitalassets/@dh/@en/@ps/documents/digitalasset/dh_113645.pdf

Department of Health (2011) *Access to the NHS by Foreign Nationals – Government response to the consultation,* Norwich: The Stationery Office; website accessed 18 March 2011: http://www.dh.gov.uk/publications

Downing, M.H. (1999) *Primary Health Care for Asylum Seekers in Dover and the Impact of Asylum Seekers on the Local Community,* unpublished report for Channel Primary Care Group

East Kent Health Authority (2000) *Health Improvement Programme 2000–2003,* Dover: EKHA.

Gatrad, A.R. (1994) 'Muslim Customs surrounding Death, Bereavement, Post-Mortem Examinations and Organ Transplants', *British Medical Journal,* **309**: 521–23.

General Practitioners Committee (GPC) (2011) *Overseas visitors accessing NHS primary medical services: Guidance for GPs*, GPC, February 2011.

Health Protection Agency (2011) *Migrant Health Guide*:
http://www.hpa.org.uk/MigrantHealthGuide/ (website accessed 18 March 2011).

Henley, A. (1979) *Asian Patients in Hospital and at Home*, Tunbridge Wells: Pitman Medical Publishing Co. Ltd.

Hopkins, A. and Bahl, V. (1993) *Access to Health Care for People from Black and Ethnic Minorities*, London: Royal College of Physicians.

Joly, D. (1995) *Britannia's Crescent: Making a Place for Muslims in British Society*, Aldershot: Avebury Press.

Karmi, G. (1996) *The Ethnic Health Handbook*, Oxford: Blackwell Science Ltd.

Karmi, G. (1998) 'Refugees' in Rawaf, S. and Bahl, V. (eds), *Assessing Health Needs of People from Ethnic Minority Groups*, London: Royal College of Physicians and the Faculty of Public Health Medicine.

Karseras, P. and Hopkins, E. (1987) *British Asians: Health in the Community (Topics In Community Health)*, London: Scutari Press

Kubba, A. (1998) 'Sexual and reproductive health' in Rawaf, S. and Bahl, V. (eds), *Assessing Health Needs of People from Ethnic Minority Groups*, London: Royal College of Physicians and the Faculty of Public Health Medicine.

McAvoy, B.R. and Donaldson, L.J. (eds) (1990) *Health Care for Asians*, Oxford: Oxford University Press.

Neile, E. (1997) 'Control for Black and Ethnic Minority Women: a Meaningless Pursuit', in Kirkham, M.J. and Perkins, E.R. (eds) *Reflections on Midwifery*, London: Baillière Tindall.

NHS Confederation (1998) *Composite Directory of NHS Ethnic Health Unit Projects*, London: NHS Confederation.

Office of National Statistics (ONS) (2002a) *Minority Ethnic Groups in the UK*, London: ONS; website accessed 19 March 2011: http://www.statistics.gov.uk/pdfdir/meg1202.pdf

Office of National Statistics (ONS) (2002b) *The Census 2001 (total population of UK)*, London: ONS; website accessed 19 March 2011: http://www.statistics.gov.uk/census2001/demographic_uk.asp

Office of National Statistics (ONS) (2002c) *The Census 2001 (population of England)*, London: ONS; website accessed 19 March 2011: http://www.statistics.gov.uk/census2001/pop2001/england.asp

Office of National Statistics (ONS) (2002d) *The Census 2001 (Ethnicity and Religion in England and Wales)*, London: ONS; website accessed 19 March 2011: http://www.statistics.gov.uk/census2001/profiles/commentaries/ethnicity.asp

Oram, J.J. (1997) *Caring for the Fourth Age*, London: Armelle Press.

Parekh, B. (2000) *The Parekh Report: the Future of Multi-Ethnic Britain*, London: Profile Books.

Radha, V. and Mohan, V. (2007) *Genetic predisposition to type 2 diabetes among Asian Indians*, website accessed 20 March 2011: http://www.ncbi.nlm.nih.gov/pubmed/174

Raleigh, V.S., Kiri, V., and Balarajan, R. (1997) 'Variations in Mortality from Diabetes Mellitus, Hypertension, and Renal Disease in England and Wales by Country of Birth', *Health Trends*, **28**: 122–27.

Rawaf, S. and Bahl, V. (eds) (1998) *Assessing Health Needs of People from Ethnic Minority Groups*, London: Royal College of Physicians and the Faculty of Public Health Medicine

The Runnymede Trust (1997) *Islamophobia: a Challenge for us all*, London: The Runnymede Trust.

Secretary of State for Health (SSfH) (1992) White Paper – *The Health of the Nation*, London: HMSO.

Secretary of State for Health (SSfH) (1997) White Paper – *The New NHS: Modern, Dependable*, London: HMSO.

Secretary of State for Health (SSfH) (2010) White Paper – *Equity and excellence: Liberating the NHS*, Norwich: The Stationery Office.

Skills for Health (Skills Academy for Health Core Learning Unit) (2011) *Respect for People – Equality and Diversity* e-learning programme; website accessed 20 March 2011: http://www.corelearningunit.com/index.php?id=2.6

SLEH (NLH Specialist Library for Ethnicity & Health) (2008) *Turning Evidence into Action – Ethnicity Data*: website accessed 20 March 2011: http://www.library.nhs.uk/ethnicity/viewResource.aspx?resid=296206&code=64d3ba0562c433735b2de685e9ce5dab

Spector, R.E. (1991) *Cultural Diversity in Health and Illness*, East Norwalk, Connecticut: Appleton and Lange.

Squires, A.J. (ed.) (1991) *Multicultural Health Care and Rehabilitation of Older People*, London: Baillière Tindall.

Timmins, S. (2000) *Sensitive and Responsive...?* (an investigation into the ability of general medical practice in East Kent to deliver primary health care which is appropriately sensitive to the needs of minority ethnic and religious patient groups), MSc dissertation, Interprofessional Health and Community Studies, Canterbury Christ Church University (unpublished).

Tovey, P. (ed.) (2000) *Contemporary Primary Care – the Challenges of Change*, Buckingham: Open University Press.

Watson, J.L. (ed.) (1977) *Between Two Cultures: Migrants and Minorities in Britain*, Oxford: Blackwell Publishers.

Weller, B. (1991) 'Nursing in a multicultural world', *Nursing Standard* **5**(30): 31–32.

World Health Organization (1978) *Declaration of Alma Ata*. International Conference on Primary Health Care, Alma Ata, USSR, 6–12 December 1978.

Further reading

Government Equalities Office (2010) *The Equality Act, 2010*, Norwich: The Stationery Office; website accessed 18 March 2011: http://www.dh.gov.uk/publications

Greenstreet, W. (ed.) (2006) *Integrating Spirituality in Health and Social Care*, Oxford: Radcliffe Publishing Ltd.

Hinnells, J.R. (1998) *A New Handbook of Living Religions*, 2nd edition, Harmondsworth: Penguin Books Ltd.

Hollins, S. (2009) *Religions, Culture and Healthcare*, Oxford: Radcliffe Publishing Ltd.

Narayanasamy, A. (2001) *Spiritual Care: a practical guide for nurses and health care practitioners*, Trowbridge: Cromwell Press.

National Association of Health Authorities & Trusts (NAHAT), (1996) *Spiritual Care in the NHS*, Birmingham: NAHAT.

NHS Blood and Transplant Service (2009) *Organ donation and religious perspectives*, leaflet ref ODR036, NHS Blood and Transfusion Service.

National NHS Information Governance Board for Health and Social Care (NIGB) (2011)*The Care Record Guarantee*, public information booklet for patients, London, NIGB, ref 4713, January 2011.

Index